Safeguarding the Heart

Safeguarding the Heart

*A Buddhist Response to Suffering
and September 11*

Yifa

Lantern Books • New York
A Division of Booklight Inc.

2002
Lantern Books
One Union Square West, Suite 201
New York, NY 10003

Printed in the United States of America

Library of Congress Cataloging-in-Publication Data

Yifa.
   Safeguarding the heart : a Buddhist response to suffering and
September 11 / Yifa.
        p. cm.
   ISBN 1-59056-034-5 (alk. paper)
   1. Suffering—Religious aspects—Buddhism. 2. Terrorism—Religious
aspects—Buddhism. 3. September 11 Terrorist Attacks, 2001. 4.
Buddhism—Doctrines. I. Title.
   BQ4235 .Y54 2002
   294.3'422—dc21
                                                    2002006011

Life with suffering and happiness
Is full;
Life with success and failure
Is reasonable;
Life with gain and loss
Is fair;
Life with birth and death
Is natural.

—Master Hsing Yun
42. *Humble Table, Wise Fare*

To Master Hsing Yun

for teaching me the Dharma

❧ Acknowledgments

I WOULD LIKE to thank Master Hsing Yun, whose wisdom is my inspiration on the spiritual path, and all those at the Fo Guang Shan temple in Taiwan and Hsi Lai University in Los Angeles for all their kindness and support over the years. I would also like to thank my two spiritual sisters, Venerable Chueh Chao and Venerable Miao Chueh, who work with me at the Greater Boston Buddhist Cultural Center. Because of their support, I am able to travel frequently. To Martin Krasney, whom I respect and admire a great deal, and who spent considerable time going through the whole manuscript and provided very thoughtful insights on how to improve it, as well as my friends Art DelVesco and Toinette Lippe for their wise comments and cogent criticism, my deepest gratitude. I would also like to acknowledge the support of Robert Oxnam. My deepest gratitude goes to Zhi-Chuang Liang of Oklahoma University, and to Michael and Rose, who helped me with the transcription of tapes from my series of lectures at university campuses in Oklahoma. And I am also glad to see the growing Buddhist Community in Oklahoma led by Dr. Wayne Stein and Tomo Koizumi at Oklahoma Central University. Thanks also to Professor Colin Blakemore, who provided me with essential information about Clive Wearing. And my sincere appreciation to Sister Meg Funk for a sisterhood that runs deeper and truer than any doctrinal differences. Finally, my thanks goes to Gene Gollogly and Martin Rowe of Lantern Books, for their encouragement of, and belief in, my writing, and for their help in editing.

✿ Table of Contents

❧ Preface

THIS BOOK WAS written in the months immediately following the destruction of the Twin Towers of the World Trade Center, a section of the Pentagon, and the jet plane in Pennsylvania on September 11, 2001. When I had originally thought of writing a book, I had intended to discuss Buddhist ideas about the self and the mind as an introduction to Buddhist thought. However, as I explored these ideas in the wake of the tragedy, the issue of suffering kept on reappearing, and I realized that this core tenet of Buddhism was tied intimately to our understanding of the self and the mind and could form the heart of a new writing project.

I was in Taiwan when I first heard about the disaster. I turned on the television and saw the two towers of the World Trade Center burning. Immediately I tried to call friends in New York, but the lines were very busy and I could not get through. I called Art DelVesco, a friend in Austin, Texas. We were both watching CNN and talking on our phone. (Now that we live in a "global village," we can witness the same scene even thousands of miles apart.)

My first response to this incident was that America would need healing. And when I saw the towers collapse, I felt my heart collapsing with them. I felt as though I was one of the people inside the buildings. I tried to imagine the impossible decisions those people faced that day: whether to jump to certain death or be burned alive; what they should say to their loved ones in their last phone calls; how they were to find their way out of the buildings, almost buried alive by the steel and the dust, with bodies falling and breaking on the ground around them. These are decisions I hope no one will have to face again.

At the end of the phone conversation between Art and myself, I said to myself, "God bless America." Many people might think that that is an odd thing for a Buddhist to say. But my request for blessing from God was an instinctive reaching-out for some comfort for a stricken country.

As much as I knew that America would need healing, however, I also sensed that this tragedy was not just an American tragedy. It was not a tragedy only for Christianity, or for Islam, for the rich nations or the poor. It was a tragedy for the whole world. In that regard, we are all in need of healing. Still, I felt then, as I feel now, that the events of September 11 do not require just healing; they require understanding. We need to find out the larger dimensions behind the event. In addition, as the time between the event and the present increases, as tragedies continue to occur—at least in terms of numbers of deaths—then we need to contextualize the suffering of that day within the continuum of the ongoing suffering of our individual and collective experiences as human beings. Such work not only brings about healing and understanding but may lead to transformation.

What this book, therefore, sets out to do is to explore September 11 in the light of central Buddhist conceptions. I begin by exploring impermanence, conditional existence, the laws of cause and effect, and karma referring to the events of September 11. I then move on, in the second part of the book, to a more general examination of the mind and self, since both are crucial to an understanding of why we suffer. I also elucidate some of the ways by which Buddhism organizes our modes of suffering. Finally, I look at some of the means at our disposal to lessen the effect of trauma on us and to foster tranquility within us and in the world around us.

In choosing September 11 as an example and focusing point, I hope to show how deeply and broadly the events of that day cast light on fundamental Buddhist truths about the nature of our existence, our obligations to our fellow beings, and the heart of our response to cruelty and misery. Even though the memory of what happened that day may fade a little, and events in the world may supersede or alter our feelings about and understanding of that event, I believe that September 11 offers all of us a chance to reflect deeply on why there is so much suffering in the world.

For me, Buddhism's constant and unblinking examination of the reasons for suffering is why I felt this book might be, at the very least, a gesture toward the healing and understanding that need to take place if we are to learn and grow from this terrible experience. My book does not pretend to contain the answer to the many different "whys" those people died in those buildings, even though I explore the laws of cause and effect and karma and our conditional existence. Nor do I answer for all Buddhists in this response—there are many Buddhist schools and many kinds of Buddhists within those Buddhist schools. They may have responded differently. My perspective is that of a Chinese Buddhist nun who was educated and has lived in the United States for many years, who became a U.S. citizen, and who has come to respect and admire the openness, energy, and warm-heartedness of the American people.

Finally, there may be some aspects of this book that you will disagree with or find upsetting. This is understandable; the events of that day, as the consequences of all suffering, are disturbing at best and horrifying at worst. But my deepest wish is that a more honest dialogue about cause and effect may lead to a lessening of the effects of suffering on all of us.

In times of tragedy, words and religious expressions can seem hopelessly vague and empty. Yet Buddhism, I believe, can offer comfort and hope, and open up a space for us to try to understand what happened and place suffering in the context of our lives. In this way, we can better comprehend how interrelated our world is and how we can best solve its problems.

Part One
September 11

1 🌿

On Impermanence
The Collapse of the Twin Towers

I T IS A scene that will be forever etched on our memories: on a cloudless day in late summer two planes arced out of a rich blue sky and carved into two of the tallest buildings in the world. One of Buddhism's central principles, that all life is impermanent, could not have been depicted in a more dramatic or more horrific manner than it was on September 11. It seemed even more terrible because much of it felt like a dream or a movie, and yet reality kept on forcing itself back on us. No, it is not a movie or a dream, our awareness insisted on telling us. It is real.

In the aftermath of that event, we have asked ourselves many questions: Why did it have to happen? Why did the hijackers hate the United States so much? Why did so many good people have to die, and die so horribly? Where was God? How should we respond? How can we stop this happening again? How do we grieve? How do we move on?

Beyond the political and military operations that have been and continue to be carried out, these questions point to larger, more metaphysical issues that require a more internal reckoning. There are already several books that look at this event from a religious perspective, some written by Buddhists. Yet, I believe, there is a need for more to be said about September 11, especially from a Buddhist point of view, since suffering and its removal lie at the heart of Buddhism.

If there is one thing that the terrible events of September 11 have proved to us, it is that everything is impermanent. And the revelation of that could not have been more immediate or more shocking. Incredibly, in barely more than a couple of hours, two huge, seemingly indestructible buildings collapsed. The event teaches us, better than any *sutra*, or religious saying, that we are desperately fragile.

Impermanence is the direct consequence of the fact that human beings, like all things, are conditioned—that is, we are made up of components, both physical and nonphysical, that are themselves composed of other things, which are also conditioned in turn. In this way, we come into being, we stay for a while and flourish, we decay or vanish, and the cycle starts again. As the Mahanirvana Sutra states, "All phenomena and matter are subject to impermanence." This truth is of fundamental importance in understanding Buddhism's view of the world. So important is it that the

Buddha's last words are reported to have been on this very matter: "Subject to change are all things, strive on with diligence." In spite of their steel girders and deep foundations, the towers of the World Trade Center could not escape impermanence. Even they had to obey the laws of nature.

When people unfamiliar with Buddhist teachings think of impermanence, they tend to think such a doctrine is very pessimistic—everything and everyone fades and dies, nothing and no one lasts. However, I believe that the concept is neither pessimistic nor optimistic; it is just a fact. The events of September 11 have shown us, and the real world constantly reveals to us, that change is constant, and change does not always happen in ways that match our perceptions or internal desires. It is through clinging to the idea of permanence that suffering occurs. By attaching ourselves to the idea of permanence and assigning it so much worth and goodness we make the inevitable changes that things go through painful and contrary to our wishes. I am sure there are a thousand examples that come to your mind: a friend who practices a healthy lifestyle suddenly dies in a car crash or gets cancer; the partner of a relative, who has just married and looks forward to a long life, dies; the child who promised so much is lost to leukemia or another illness.

For most people impermanence seems a terrifying concept. Because of impermanence, good things go bad. Our possessions break or stop working because of impermanence. We lose our livelihoods because of impermanence. We die because of impermanence. Impermanence does not appear to be a good thing. Consequently, we all desire permanence. When I was young, I hoped I would look more mature than my years. Now that I am over forty, however, I do not want people to remind me of how old I am! Like many of us, I would like to be young forever. I do not want to face having to grow old. Permanence is deeply desirable.

This view of impermanence, however, depends on understanding the self as a defined, absolute identity. For us in the West, who are obsessed with the concept of self, the radicalism of Buddhism's teaching on impermanence is what makes Buddhism so challenging. We believe we are absolute entities, we are proud of our personalities; we identify with them and refuse to change. But we *can* change. We *can* get better, move on, try again. This is also a condition of impermanence—that we are free to change, to try to correct the former mistakes we have made, attempt to throw off the shackles of fate or poor health and economic disadvantage and change them all for the better. After all, if we could not, what would be the point of education? This is another essential lesson of Buddhism.

I realize that always keeping in mind the fact that everything is impermanent is not easy to do. Yet if we carry in our minds the idea that everything is going to change—that even though we may live with someone for sixty, seventy, even eighty years, our loved ones or we ourselves will die, or that they and we may perhaps go in an instant—then that change becomes a little easier to tolerate. Ironically, the foundation of the United States was predicated on both change and permanence. America was to be governed by the unyielding principles of individuals pursuing their destiny—words enshrined in the Declaration of Independence and the Constitution of the United States—yet the country was also the promised land for millions of immigrants from around the world who came in hopes of changing their fortunes, their culture, even their identities. The attack on those apparently rock-solid buildings of the World Trade Center, located at the center of the still-beating if battered heart of the American Dream, is a stark reminder of how dangerous it is to accept permanence and how change is not merely a fact but a law of nature.

Furthermore, the very transience of life and its vulnerability, the knowledge that the world is fragile and delicate, can help us cherish the moments when we are together with our loved ones and honor and enjoy the short amount of time we are allotted in each lifetime. Indeed, the death of something can bring about the birth of something else. It is a fundamental law of the natural world that the decomposition of matter allows other things to grow and develop. When a forest burns, there is not only the regeneration of new life, but sometimes life in even greater profusion and variety. Some forests even require fire for their regeneration. When an animal dies in the ecosystem, other animals feed on, and life forms grow out of, the dead body. In this way, the world is kept fresh and recharged. This doctrine of impermanence also offers hope to everyone living under tyranny or oppression—because even the most despotic of tyrants will die; even the greatest of empires will inevitably come to an end. The world is littered with the remnants of enormous statues to the powerful rulers of past ages that have crumbled into the desert to be dispersed by the winds or have been washed away by the tide.

The recognition of the neutrality of impermanence—an understanding that death is neither good nor bad, but merely a fact—is one of Buddhism's great gifts. It helps us grasp that the reason why we are afraid of death and suffering is not because they are too present to us but, to the contrary, because in our fear we refuse to admit they are with us. Paradoxically, only by grasping suffering and death, by holding tight to the meanings and experiences of September 11, will we be given the insight and wisdom that will help us gain equanimity.

2

On Cause and Effect

How Events Are Connected through Time

WHILE THE COLLAPSE of the Twin Towers showed how vulnerable the world we live in can be, we should not believe that the world is governed by randomness or chaos. Impermanence does not mean complete unpredictability. There are causes and conditions, and causes and conditions in the past lead to results in the present moment. If we want to know what the causes of our present condition are, then all we have to do is look at the results and traumas of our life in the past. If we want to know what will happen in the future, then all we need to do is look at our actions at this moment.

For me, the attack on September 11 illustrated how absolutely this was true. Very shortly after the event, the government and the media told us who they believed the culprits were and how they had done it. But what was less clearly articulated was *why* these events had happened.

In the weeks and months following September 11, I asked people in the United States that question. The answer I invariably received was that the United States was attacked because people are jealous of its wealth, power, and democracy. Clearly, there are elements of truth in this—the United States' great wealth and its power are a magnet to many people around the world who seek relief from the poverty and oppression of their own countries. Likewise, freedom is something we all yearn for—and the United States has indeed become a beacon of freedom for people around the world.

Yet I believe the laws of cause and effect are more complicated than that. Osama bin Laden may well have been richer than most of the people in the United States, while the alleged hijackers were men with education and standing. It seems unlikely, therefore, that it was only poverty and ignorance that led them to carry out their attack. Indeed, if it were merely poverty, then surely poorer countries would have attacked the United States long ago. Nor was it solely the lunatic expression of a medieval mindset seeking to bring down an imperial force. The hijackers and their backers were sophisticates, who, astonishingly effectively, turned an unarmed civilian jet into a weapon more powerful than the most heavily armed missile from the most well-equipped fighting force in the world. These were modern men who knew what they were doing and had the skills and the knowledge to carry out their plan.

I do not believe, therefore, that simply the wealth and power of the United States were the reasons why the country was attacked. It is my belief that there are more reasons for September 11 than jealousy or envy. American involvement during and after the Gulf War, disengagement after the Soviet army pulled out of Afghanistan, and many other geopolitical actions contributed to September 11, along with the repression and hypocrisy of several Arabic regimes, and the anger people feel over not being able to hold their unelected leaders accountable. If we single out September 11 as an aberration, the mere venting of an ancient fury, we will not see the event for what it is—an action that had causes and conditions that led up to it and that in turn has results and conditions leading out of it.

By emphasizing complexity and the laws of cause and effect, I am not trying to blame the United States for what happened. The deliberate use of terror for any purposes is clearly unjustified under any circumstances. What I am trying to point out is that any action will produce an effect. Whatever the reasons why the United States pulled out of Afghanistan after the end of the Cold War, that abandonment of the Afghans came back to haunt it. By intervening in the destabilization of the country and then not staying to help it rebuild in the early 1990s, the United States assisted in some way in *creating the conditions* for September 11. At the time of writing, it is uncertain whether it will make the

20188972

same mistake again. Likewise, by engaging with the Islamic world in the Gulf War and then failing to follow the victory over Iraq with a continuing diplomatic engagement with countries in that area, the United States was unable to dilute or divert the emergent Islamist extremism that provided Osama bin Laden and others with supporters and safe havens.

It is impossible to know what would have happened if the United States had pressured Kuwait and Saudi Arabia to encourage a more open, democratic society, or the United States had urged Saudi Arabia to stop exporting a virulent anti-Americanism in its schools and publications (a case similar to Egypt). It is impossible to know what would have happened had the United States attempted to foster democratic impulses in Iran and Iraq and not sought to destabilize either one through sanctions or arms shipments. But it is clear that the United States' support of Saddam Hussein during the Iran-Iraq war of 1980–1988 and the U.S. victory in the Gulf War came with many consequences, not all of them immediately obvious or beneficial to the United States and its allies. Likewise, Pakistan, with its democratically elected government, was considered an important ally throughout the 1990s, even as it was overtly supporting both the Taliban and the Kashmiri militants in their incursions into Indian-ruled Kashmir, and providing not only a safe haven but support for al-Qaeda. It is, indeed, ironic, that Pervez Musharraf, who has helped the United States destroy the Taliban, is unelected. Again, to say the attacks were caused by jealousy over democracy is too simple.

What is clear is that engagement with parts of the world that are saturated with ethnic, religious, and geopolitical rivalries and hatreds extending back sometimes hundreds of years is, to say the very least, dangerous. However, the answer is not—as some have argued—more isolation from the rest of the world. If nothing else, September 11 has shown us that isolationism and unilateralism are even more dangerous than engagement, because the more the United States cuts itself off from the world, the more the world will come to it. Our world is increasingly globalized. Isolationism can never be the answer, not least because at the beginning of the twenty-first century it is virtually impossible.

What, therefore, is the responsibility of the United States in defusing the danger? The answer is not, as I have heard some say, producing better propaganda. What is required is an honest sharing of the wealth, a redistribution of power, and a commitment to fostering democracy and openness throughout the world. America's greatest gift to the world has always been its promise of freedom, tolerance, pluralism, and a commitment to justice. Indeed, the words "unalienable rights" that are linked to "life, liberty, and the pursuit of happiness" in the Declaration of Independence illustrate that these freedoms are not foreign (Latin, *alienus*) and thus are open to everyone, in the United States and everywhere else. This is why the attack on freedom on September 11 was an attack on everyone's right to liberty.

So, it is important that the United States represent more fully the search for freedom and foster the means to bring that about throughout the world. Too often, it seems to me, the United States is seen as a rapacious superpower, unwilling to listen to the rest of the world, intolerant of views divergent from its own, and overly concerned with consumption. These, indeed, are caricatures; but they are caricatures that are too readily proved by many in the United States, who see many countries in the developing world as bastions of endemic corruption, terrorism, misgovernment, and knee-jerk anti-Americanism. In this way, the misunderstandings of both worlds perpetuate a cycle of perceived slights and injustices that have escalated into war. In both cases, innocent people, who merely want to get on with their lives, look after their families, and seek peace, are the victims. In both cases, ignorance and intolerance build on themselves while knowledge and understanding are considered weak or craven.

Buddhism understands that the governing principle of cause and effect demands that we understand the whole picture and not just isolate the causes and effects of our actions that we find convenient to accept. Buddhism demands that we look at the world honestly, and not just as our politicians, our parents, or our own fears tell us to do. The laws of cause and effect are ruthless and unstoppable— both for the good and for the bad—and they need to be understood very well if the negative is to be curtailed and the positive to be maximized. The laws cannot be eradicated; the actions one undertakes cannot vanish. When the causes and conditions come together, then you have to face the effects. Thus, it is incumbent on us to create healthy outcomes by setting up the causes for healthy outcomes, to create wealth by setting up the causes for wealth, and to create good people not only by creating the environment for goodness to flourish but by being good ourselves.

Of course, the laws of cause and effect often do not operate as baldly as the previous sentence might suggest. They can be subtle and profound. For instance, we can see how the positive can be maximized in the results of the World Trade Center tragedy. While what the hijackers did was unconscionable, not all the consequences of their actions were bad. People's compassion and sense of togetherness were heightened immediately after the events of September 11. We found out that what was truly valuable was not material possessions or having a lot of money; instead, we rediscovered community and courage and working for something greater than our personal safety. People took time out of their busy lives to volunteer or to reflect on how fragile life is, how we can be cut down in the middle of going about our daily business, how attached we are to trivialities and things that ultimately have no value.

We began to talk to each other and hear each other's stories. After a decade in which the heroes were dot-com millionaires and we obsessed about the private lives of celebrities, we discovered heroes who weren't famous or necessarily glamorous or rich, but epitomized courage and heroism—firefighters, police officers, emergency medical teams, volunteers, ordinary men and women. And there were larger political dimensions. We were forced to look away from the prosperity and, I might say, self-satisfaction of our lives in the United States to acknowledge the enormous suffering of many poor people around the world. Would we have dropped food shipments over Afghanistan if those planes had not struck the World Trade Center? All actions have a reaction. Perhaps the hijackers did not realize that one reaction within the United States would be compassion for the people of Afghanistan and a reawakened sense of community in America. That consequence—the beauty of countless acts of generosity, tenderness, and compassion—may be their ultimate punishment.

This analysis of the political ramifications of cause and effect is, I know, of little comfort to the individuals who lost loved ones in New York, Washington, D.C., or Afghanistan. This is why we need to unite compassion with wisdom, because wisdom can help us look at things from a more unbiased angle. When we look at events such as the Cultural Revolution in China or the terrorist attack on the World Trade Center, it is tempting to see them as merely regional conflicts, as localized tragedies. But when we have compassion we see them as more than regional. They are human tragedies.

In other words, some people think that if they have an infection, simply cutting out the infected area or severing the infected body part will solve the problem. But when we have compassion, we see the infection from the perspective of the whole body. The infection is not merely localized; the disease affects the whole body. Consequently, the whole body needs to be healed.

The connections of cause and effect through time thus require a holistic response that pays attention to history—and not merely our own. It means acknowledging the larger body that is the human family before we seek to remedy that ailing body by surgically removing a part of it. It means recognizing that we can neither engage with nor flee from the world without consequence. We are *all* connected.

3 ❧

On Interdependence

How Events Are Connected through Space

T HE LAWS OF cause and effect act through time to make every action haunt or support us in the future. In terms of the temporal results of the laws of cause and effect, as the last chapter has suggested, America's isolationist tendencies have been abruptly and violently challenged. The United States has been forced to re-engage with the Middle East peace process, to send troops into Afghanistan, and now talks about military operations in several other countries around the world.

In this regard, Buddhism's relationality—its sense that everything is dependent—stands in opposition to the doctrines of isolation and self-containment that many people in the West feel is the normal state of being. In the United States, we like to have privacy—based on the central role of private property and individual liberty as governing ideas in the laws of the country. But sometimes, that sense of the need to defend what is one's own becomes non-communication and ignorance. We do not like to know what goes on elsewhere: we stay in our nice neighborhoods and do not care about the ghettos or poor areas. Understandably perhaps, we want to protect ourselves.

Self-protection, however, as we discovered on September 11, is not enough. We can never fully isolate ourselves, never escape from dependence. What Buddhism does is teach us to recognize our interdependence and then instruct us in taking responsibility not only for ourselves but for the whole society. What happens in the ghettos and poor countries affects us by making us fearful. Our lives, therefore, are conditioned by fear in the same way that they would be if we drove through a neighborhood and were worried about being the victim of a drive-by shooting. Fear is fear, whatever the probability of its being justified.

Buddhism's concern is not simply with our individual lives or the lives of those who live around us. It is not limited by the desires of the nation state or the wishes of the geopolitical regions. Buddhism is not content to rest at this planet. As a sutra says, a thousand solar systems make up the extent of a small world; a thousand small worlds make up the extent of an intermediate world; and a thousand middle worlds make up the extent of the big world. This is what is meant in Buddhism by the "three layers of the thousand worlds." In this way, Buddhism seeks to convey its belief that there are unlimited worlds in the universe, each of them exerting an influence on our individual lives and each of our individual lives exerting an influence on the innumerable universes.

If we perceive existence in such a way, it can only teach us to be both humble and awesomely aware of our responsibility. Buddhism argues that everything we do has a consequence. Whether the cause is good or bad, whether it is in thought or deed, it always leads to an effect. Sometimes, the action is relatively inconsequential: if I knock into the table, I feel pain. Why? Because when I exert force upon the table there is a reaction against my hand and I feel pain. This is the consequence, a punishment, if you will, for my initial action. In a similar way, a car moves because the energy it releases creates thrust that pushes the car forward. To adapt the maxim from physics: Every reaction has an equal, if not always opposite, reaction. And we are in fact a tiny presence in the huge pushes and pulls of cause and effect throughout the universe—a thought that should encourage humility.

By looking at things holistically, by placing oneself in the shoes of another, one has the opportunity to grasp the spatial dimension of cause and effect and to act more prudently to maximize the good and minimize the bad consequences of one's actions. The world did it in the aftermath of World War II in Western Europe, where broken societies were given the money and the resources to move from being seedbeds of dictatorship to seedbeds of democracy; the United States did the same in Japan. But it takes time, patience, and presence.

After September 11, the United States in particular and the world in general has an opportunity to replace the old divisions and longstanding grievances and subsequent outrages with a different set of causes and effects.

The same is the case with losing the recognition that we are independent beings. We like to think we are self-sufficient, self-determined, self-motivating. We believe that we are entitled to certain things, that we deserve what we want, because we are self-contained. But we all have to live and work together. Simply to get through life requires cooperation and mutual interdependence. When we are babies, we are utterly dependent upon others, and this dependence in fact continues throughout our life. Our physical body and feelings depend on our contact with the outside world, a world where our memory and experience also interact. From the interpersonal to the international, we all rely on another or others to help us achieve what we want to achieve. Shops rely on us to buy products from them. Countries require other countries for trade. If we can truly realize this—in our individual lives, our communal lives, and between the nations—then the suffering to which we are all subject will be diminished.

4 🦚
On Karma
The Ties That Bind

WE HAVE SEEN how Buddhism argues that we are all interconnected and live interdependently. The question that now poses itself is, what is the factor that binds us together and reveals our interconnectedness? Buddhists understand this phenomenon through the concept of *karma.* As we all live interdependently or interconnectedly, we share the results from the collective karma. Whatever our feelings about what happened on September 11, the Buddhist understanding of the event is that there was some sort of karmic connection—collective or shared karma and individual karma. Similarly, we all experienced or witnessed the attack of September 11, even if to different extents, and we were all affected by this attack directly or indirectly. There is a karmic connection for all of us. As an obvious example, we all now have to undergo much more inconvenience when we go through the airport security checking.

All of the people who died—the people on the plane, the hijackers, the firefighters, police, and workers in the building—were connected. This may seem a strange statement, but on further reflection it shows itself to be true. The hijackers had their minds on the buildings. The people who worked in these buildings—the very symbol of world capitalism, of prestige, power, and status—also had their minds, in some way, on the buildings. A young man I know who is finishing his Ph.D. in biochemistry at Harvard told me that he was going to work in some company in the World Trade Center—a symbol of prestige in his field, too. But now he cannot even bear to work in New York.

The place meant very different things to these different people, but nevertheless it somehow bound them together. The terrorists focused on the World Trade Center and the Pentagon not because they were random buildings, but because they had invested them with an idea of power and importance. Likewise, the horror that was felt around the world at the attacks was not solely because of the loss of innocent life and the manner in which that life was taken. It was because these buildings to all of us also represented the confidence and strength of the United States. The terrorists knew they were destroying much more than buildings, and our response to the attack has confirmed it. This is one dimension of karma.

This concept of karma is hard for any of us to take—especially if, like so many of us, we are wrapped up in the pain of loss and seeking for some understanding of why tragedy happened to us and how we can bring the perpetrators of the act of terror to justice. Buddhism may, at times like these, seem a little unyielding in its honest attempt to respond to the hardest experiences of our life. Yet I believe that a true understanding of karma offers a way forward for justice as well as healing.

Karma originally means "act" or "volition." Karma always has a cause and it always has an effect. There are three aspects to karma: the thought processes that lead you to action; the actual karma of carrying out the action; and the way you talk about the action. I remember once seeing an advertisement on TV that had the tagline, "Whatever the path you walk on, you will always leave a trace." This touches on the meaning of karma, except that I always say that it is not only the path you walk on that bears your imprint; even *thinking* about the path or *talking* about it leaves some trace, some energy. This is why we do anything—because we think about it. These thoughts accumulate mental karma and lead you to the place where physical karma is acted out. This is why people with different karmic thoughts were drawn to the World Trade Center.

I want to make it very clear here that I am not saying that the firefighters or police officers, or the workers in the buildings, or the passengers on the planes who were not the hijackers, *wanted* to die. I am not saying they were drawn by karmic thoughts on that particular day in a perverse kind of death wish. I am not saying that everyone had the same thoughts as the hijackers. What Buddhism teaches is that it is important to look at any incident, including this tragic event, as not just an isolated, single happening. As I have suggested, Buddhism asks us to expand time and space and follow causes and effects.

The hijackers who took over the planes and rammed them into the Twin Towers and the Pentagon did not merely act on impulse. They had reasons; they had something on their minds. Over the years, these men had grown up in a certain environment and culture, within a certain faith with a certain worldview, that had led them to that place at that time.

Furthermore, the worldviews and cultures and environments in which they grew up were also not isolated. They were affected by other worldviews, cultures, and environments, which were in turn affected by others of perhaps a different kind. The destructive thoughts that went through the hijackers' minds were an accumulation of many thoughts—perhaps conflicted, contradictory, and blinkered thoughts—about what Islam meant, what the West was, what the value of life is, and what death leads to. We ourselves may even share some of these beliefs. Consequently, the perpetrator and victim were linked through the accumulation of all the conditioned thoughts that led to that particular moment. The fact that the terrorists used, by way of a weapon, a plane that was built in the United States by U.S. workers, and was used to kill people who were either U.S. citizens or attached to the U.S. in some way, reveals how bound we all are in the karma of the event. When we look at the event in this way, we see how the event, as I said in my preface, was not simply an American tragedy, or a tragedy of the relationship between Islam and Christianity, but a world tragedy.

In spite of such connections made between those who committed murder and those who were murdered, the ultimate question we always ask ourselves when confronted by tragedy remains a great mystery: "Why did good people have to die in such a terrible way or in such a terrible location?" To try and offer at least some kind of answer to this, we might look at the deaths of the police officers and firefighters, as well as the people they were trying to rescue, in another way.

Buddhism venerates individuals who work their many lives seeking to remove the causes of suffering and karma through their presence and actions so that all beings may be released from suffering. They are called bodhisattvas, and they vow to help people not only on earth and in heaven, but also in hell. Most people who are reborn in hell are there because of the accumulation of bad karma. However, there are some beings who are reborn in hell because that is their vow. These beings are known as Ksitigarbha bodhisattvas, and they are beings who vow to save all the sentient beings in hell.

A Buddhist story tells of a disciple who came to his master with a question.

"Master, after you die, where are you going to be reborn?"

"In hell," the master replied.

The disciple was puzzled. "Why would someone as spiritually refined and cultivated as yourself be reborn in hell?"

"If I am not reborn in hell," the master replied, "then who is going to save you?"

I recall reading an article from a survivor of the Twin Towers attack who described the scene in the stairwell as she exited the building. She said that as she and others were making their way down, they saw the firefighters "with hoses in their hands, sweat on their faces, and stepping upward. This will be the scene that left the scar in my mind forever." Imagining this picture, I believe that the firefighters and police officers were Ksitigarbha bodhisattvas, committing themselves to rescuing people in the midst of hell. This was their karmic connection.

Some might say that karma in some way absolves perpetrators from their acts of harm because it makes all of us somehow involved—we all like to believe that we can get away with doing something bad if we can. According to Buddhism, however, if you do something good or bad, there is *always* a reaction. This will be recorded as your karma or karmic force. So we have to be aware of what we are saying all the time, because this karmic force will accumulate in our consciousness and lead to reincarnation or rebirth. In this way, Buddhism, although it talks of the impermanence of the self, is not about absolving individuals from their actions. Far from it! Because we are interdependent, all our actions have consequences. Buddhism, therefore, teaches the utmost respect for others, precisely because we *are* those others. Consequently, the serial killer will receive punishment in the next lifetime through the karma he accumulated in this one.

I once met a man who told me he did not believe in life after death. He believed that the physical body simply faded away, leaving nothing behind. I asked him whether he believed in justice and universal truth. What, I asked, if a serial killer, who had murdered a lot of people, escaped the law, led a long life, and died peacefully, unpunished for his crime? Would you be willing to accept this, I asked the man. He did not have an answer, but I believe that he would not have accepted the answer that good goes unrewarded and evil goes unpunished in the universe.

Indeed, it may seem shocking that the laws of karma mean that some people in the World Trade Center survived while others perished. However, we do not know the karmic reasons why they had to die, since karma operates throughout time—into the past, within the present, and into the future. Moreover, karma functions like a plant. A plant can blossom once a year, or may live for only two years, or every year. Each plant blossoms at different times and under different conditions; plants that seem dead may spring to life while others may bloom at the point of death. People who do bad things in this life may not receive retribution in this life, but will experience suffering in the next life. People who do good things may suffer because of what they did in previous lives. Yet, just as the laws of cause and effect are immutable, so is the natural law of justice. Good deeds will create good karma; bad deeds bad karma.

As I mentioned earlier, one of the probably unintended consequences of the terrible events of September 11 was that we in the developed world had to turn our gaze to those in the developing world who have nothing. The event that centered so particularly on three buildings and four planes in the United States has forced this country to look out at the great sea of suffering that engulfs billions of people around the world. Perhaps these terrible events were not only the coming to fruition of bad karma—the culmination of lots of individual negative acts that ended in the hijacking of those planes—but the ripening of good karma, a mobilization of the world for compassion and justice, to root out the causes of the suffering that created the hijackers.

Thus, out of great evil can come great good, and those who wished to destroy humanity and tear peoples apart could have their wishes completely inverted by allowing humanity to rebuild and come together—if we act without vengeance. We have seen the pictures of the children in Afghanistan, orphaned, starving, never having known peace or security. Are they our enemy? Was it they who drove the planes into the twin towers of the World Trade Center and the Pentagon?

Of course not. They are innocent, just as every child is innocent. What we must protect against, however, is their becoming the unintended victims of our karmic actions. If we act in any situation, whether as a nation or as individuals merely with vengeance and our acts of violence in turn breed another generation of desperate young people who are willing to shed their lives because of what happened to them, then the hijackers of September 11 will have succeeded. So, we are all potential or actual victims and we are all potential or actual perpetrators. Buddhism's challenge is to turn bad karma into good.

5 🌿

On Justice

The Quest for Justice in the Aftermath of Tragedy

IN MY LAST chapter I mentioned the sense of justice, and you may be wondering how Buddhism conceives of justice. Justice is a function of natural law and, like karma, works in the past, present, and future. Put simply, if an action comes from good intentions, then there will be a good reaction. If the action comes from bad intentions, then there will a bad reaction. The universe acts as justice itself, and the universe is never compromised.

For instance, if we damage the earth, the earth will be destroyed, and so will we. Some people may get rich in the process, but their descendants will suffer the consequences of their actions. Good intention in the case of the World Trade

Center tragedy would mean working for peace rather than mere revenge; bad intention would mean working for revenge and a return to isolationism and ignorance. The bad karma of the terrorists will be lessened by the good actions of bringing aid and comfort to the poor and desperate, and thus seeding a positive association in people's minds. The bad karma of the terrorists will be exacerbated if the cycle of violence is merely perpetuated, enhancing grievances and crushing hopes.

In this regard, the operation of the world is the operation of justice. It is not a function of human justice, because human justice is conditioned, bound by the context of our background, society, cultural ideas, etc. This is why justice needs to be thought of as separate from punishment. Punishment is what the hijackers wished to do to America—to punish the United States for its perceived transgressions. The belief in punishment as justice merely perpetuates a cycle of more punishment as justice. But true justice is not about punishment; it is about being aware of cause and effect.

Justice is absolutely impartial—it is merely the sum of good and bad actions operating within the universe. However, we can model human laws so that more good is generated than bad. This is why one of the principle ideas of Buddhism is nonviolence. Nonviolence means not doing anything to make bad situations worse as well as not creating bad situations. By creating laws that exacerbate the good, rather than simply creating laws to stop people doing bad things, you create situations in which less violence is needed because there are fewer situations where violence is generated. But karmic laws are complicated and life is never easy, and our choices are not always yes or no. We have to constantly weigh our options, always bearing in mind the need to foster the good and to limit the bad.

Laws should be created to nurture the well being of humans. Unfortunately, some people have made laws to punish or destroy other human beings rather than bring about justice. I think this is opposite to the intent of natural law. The law should help people by removing the conditions for suffering and negative actions and creating the conditions for justice. But we all get caught up in legalism, bureaucracy, and technology. At times fear and material things overwhelm us and we lose perspective of what is true and meaningful.

So, like our response to suffering, the application of justice needs to be looked at holistically. We need to try to see the situation from many angles before we make judgments. Only this way can we make sense of why someone can kill another person and yet not be punished for it in this lifetime. Buddhists know that that person will pay a heavy karmic debt in future lifetimes. Furthermore, we can seek to understand the wrongdoer's action by looking at the conditions that led him to kill another person, and thereby not only provide an apt punishment for the individual, but also seek to make sure that such conditions are not ripe for more people to do the same thing. A question that might be asked at this point is how we should make judgments about what is wrong. How do we bring people who do bad things to justice? Indeed, what is justice when everything is conditioned?

Buddhism acknowledges that we have a mind and that the mind makes judgments. Judgments in and of themselves may not be inherently bad or good. Like all actions, they have a cause and effect, and thus can create good or bad effects. Now, clearly judgment is necessary for our survival. We tell children not to touch fire because they will be burned. Or we tell them not to go swimming in deep water because they could drown, or that they should not eat dog food because it was not designed for human beings. Judgment here is based on our knowledge of the effect that putting your hand in a fire might have and the child's ignorance of it. We project an effect into the future because we understand the cause of harm.

But these judgments, while sensible, are still conditioned, a result of some form of experience or cultural understanding. There is nothing inherent in these judgments that separates them from a judgment, for instance, that black people are criminals, or people with yellow skins are materialistic, or women are weak. These are prejudices that also depend on our projections. They are judgments conditioned by our cultural background, our family's mores, our sense of ourselves.

Buddhism holds that all people are the same—all conditioned, interdependent beings—no matter who they are, their gender, color, religion, sexual orientation, or state of mind. During the course of our lives we are exposed to different conditions, all of which have causes and all of which have consequences. So we need to be careful that our loving care for protecting our children and telling them to watch out for strangers does not merge with our cultural conditioning that they should watch out for strangers with different-colored skin or different religious views. More facts or knowledge may not guarantee that we become aware of our conditioning. Only wisdom can do that.

Thus justice means recognizing our prejudices and understanding our self-serving motivations and working for the benefit of all beings. This is a great challenge—especially when confronted with horrors such as September 11. Nonetheless, if we are to stop violence and perpetuate peace, we must set ourselves the hard challenges.

6 ✻

On Faith

The Distinction between Religion and Truth

WHEN WE THINK about the tragedy of September 11, we immediately see that the event was categorized as a religious struggle. Indeed, so much suffering in the world, both in the past and at the moment, has a religious cast. Religion, one might go so far as to say, seems to be the cause of so much suffering!

Yet religion is merely the path that helps us to explore the truth within. It is, in essence, a means to an end. However, throughout history, as we see today, countless people have viewed religion not as a sacred path to the truth, but as truth itself. And yet no one religion can be equated with truth itself. Each of the world's major religions has a history, a time span; but the truth cannot have a time span. By definition, truth cannot be conditional or temporally bound. The truths that religions seek and espouse are eternal, but the religions themselves are historically fixed in time.

As a Zen parable describes it, the master or teacher instructs by pointing a finger at the moon. To cling to one's own belief as the truth itself—or even as the sole means to the truth—is like clinging to the master's finger only, without seeing the moon at all. However, even the moon itself is not to be equated with the truth. The truth is found only when we make the mind as clean as a mirror, to reflect the moon and all its surroundings within it. To clean this mirror-like surface, we need to remove the murky illusion of self that divides our world, to lift ourselves out of the categories with which we frame our lives. An example of this is in the Diamond Sutra, where the Buddha tells his disciples, "My teaching is like the raft you shall abandon after you cross the river. You shall not carry it on your shoulders after you get on the shore." In other words, religion is a tool to reach enlightenment; after enlightenment or true wisdom is reached, religion is no longer necessary.

Communication and dialogue among members of differing religious frameworks is a major step toward the overcoming of artificial boundaries, the removal of illusions and prejudices within us, and the search for common ground and universal truths. We need to respect each other's faiths. For instance, the founder of Humanistic Buddhism, Master Hsing Yun, begins his prayer with: "Buddha, God, Jesus...." He believes it is possible to have more than one belief. Indeed, religious pluralism can help us avoid the kind of blind faith that misleads some people to destroy other lives along with their own and believe they will go to heaven.

I do not mean, however, to suggest that we destroy the boundaries and differences that distinguish our various traditions and religious beliefs. Rather, it is hoped that we might seek a way to transcend such categories in search of common truths, to remain confident that no truth can call itself by that name if it fears being questioned. On the contrary, the greatest truths are born of constant seeking. And yet, such seeking does not mean we turn our backs even for a moment on our own unique religions—just as seeking transcendent truths should never mean one stops working among all people of the world to better their conditions. We need to transcend our everyday categories—not to abandon them, but to discover higher truths, greater beauty, and apply this knowledge to our everyday world.

When one realizes that the self and the various categories it creates, including religion itself, are, in a sense, merely arbitrary boundaries that can be transcended, one begins to see the world as a far more hopeful place. Fundamentally, we are all united—Christians, Muslims, Hindus, Jews, and Buddhists alike. To heal ourselves we must transcend our differences and atone for our prejudices—for to *atone* is to be *at one*. In fact, we need to consider the possibility that unless we do transcend religion as a category, we cannot truly hope to practice the ideals that religion professes to embody. When we think of the world after September 11, the perils of thinking only in terms of the superiority of our own religious tradition become very clear.

7 ✻

On Death and the Afterlife
Are We in Heaven or Hell?

HOW WE DIE is a very important feature of Buddhism. Buddhism demands that we pay great attention to the nature and balance of our mind throughout life so that when we die, we experience peace and can unattach ourselves from our body. Even so, Buddhism recognizes that the actual moment of dying, while it may feel as though we are in hell, is only a short experience in the span of our many lives.

Buddhism suggests that there are six realms that govern existence. The lowest realm—or the realm that is most affected by bad karmic conditions—is the region of hell. The next lowest is that of ghosts or spirits. The realm karmically above the realm of ghosts is that of the animals. The next realm is that of the Asuras, or titanic gods or demons, followed by that of human beings. The final realm is that of heaven, or the realm of the gods. Unlike Judaism and Christianity, which see heaven and hell as final destinations, Buddhism believes that an individual goes through all of these dimensions depending on his or her karmic history. So, for Buddhism, neither heaven nor hell is necessarily your ultimate dimension. Indeed, heaven is not necessarily the place you end up when you are completely good and hell where you end up when you have been irredeemably bad. In heaven, for instance, it is possible to experience a surfeit of wealth and joy and so become lax in the continued cultivation of wisdom—the ultimate aim of all Buddhists. Similarly, as we noted with the Ksitigarbha bodhisattva, good souls operate in hell as a way to rescue those who have ended up in the lowest realm.

This conception of existence—governed by movement through different realms throughout our lives—means that at any moment we are surrounded by those on their way to hell and those on their way to heaven and, most importantly, by bodhisattvas who are working all the time to enable us to change our lives for the better. Just as September 11 showed us that even in the midst of absolute hell there were great souls—in the shape of firefighters and police officers—who gave their lives for others, so Buddhism tells us that their legacy of good is not finite. Even now they are working to create good karma, by allowing us to make our lives similarly meaningful and compassionate.

In December 2001, a number of firefighters who had lost colleagues and family in the World Trade Center tragedy went to Afghanistan to help feed orphans at the Alaodin orphanage on the outskirts of Kabul. According to the BBC, when the firefighter Joe Higgins, whose brother was killed in the World Trade Center, was asked how he felt now that he was in the country that had sheltered the people who killed his colleagues, he did not express vindictiveness or anger. He did not even say that he had experienced a kind of catharsis or feelings of peace. "Humbling," is how he described his reaction. "We are here to show that we do not hold Afghan people responsible." Many of the children whom the firefighters served had never heard of New York. Now, of course, they have, and their experience is a positive one. That is a good karmic action that will have effects for generations to come. Even in the hell of starvation and deprivation that is present-day Afghanistan, the bodhisattvas are working.

What we need to understand is that we can individually make a hell of heaven and a heaven of hell through our actions. Furthermore, by not attaching ego to the actions and not concentrating on the effects of our good deeds—by being, like the firefighter, humbled—we can make a difference.

I have a friend who is the founder of an animal protectionist organization called Last Chance for Animals. One day, recalling the pledge all bodhisattvas make, he said to me, "Yifa, I vow to save all the sentient beings in the world."

"That's good you have vowed to do that," I told him. "But do not expect it to happen."

"Why?" he asked.

"Because," I replied, "animals, just like human beings, are unlimited. Their suffering is endless."

But my animal protection friend is not going to change, nor should he. Like a good bodhisattva, he will keep working to stop the suffering of all sentient beings.

Another time I went to a doctor's clinic. "You are very good," I said to the doctor, "but you never run out of patients. Even the ones you have cured come back to you again. Do you ever expect to finish healing all the patients in the world?" His answer was, of course, no. Yet, he will still turn up for work tomorrow, ready to try to cure those patients lined up outside his office.

Many of us are overwhelmed when confronted with the suffering of the world. Even as a Buddhist nun I often feel swamped by that suffering. We wonder what we can do. We feel paralyzed. When I was talking with the animal advocate and the doctor, I was not arguing that they should stop trying to alleviate suffering. Far from it: Buddhists make it our central goal. What I meant, however, is that we should go about alleviating suffering with humility and a lack of attachment. This lack of attachment is not a lack of caring or some sort of indifference. What it means is that we should not attach ego or pride or greed to the action.

There is a story attributed to the writer Loren Eiseley about a man who one day was walking along the seashore. On the sand he saw countless starfish, thousands upon thousands of them, which had been carried by the tide onto the beach and were dying in the heat of the sun. The man felt helpless at seeing all these bodies piling up. Then he saw a girl picking starfish up and one by one throwing them back into the sea. Going up to the child, the man asked her what she was doing.

"I am rescuing the starfish," said the girl.

"But there are thousands and thousands of them," said the man. "Do you think what you are doing is going to make a difference?"

The girl looked at him and pointed to the starfish in her hand. "It makes a difference to *this* starfish," she said.

This story points up a central truth illuminated in Buddhism. Without hope for reward and, in some way, acknowledging the hopelessness of her task, the child yet felt compassion for each individual sentient being she came across. She did not see life as a collective, and nor was she overwhelmed and paralyzed by the enormous suffering taking place on the beach. Instead, she focused on what she *could* do and saved those individuals she *could* save, because she knew that each of the starfish lives mattered to each individual starfish, and that in the end was what counted. Likewise, the Buddhist, as a bodhisattva, takes on the task of rescuing all sentient beings and postponing his or her own liberation from the cycle of death–birth–rebirth, so that, in his or her own particular way, he or she can throw individual starfish back into the water.

There is an additional component that needs to be understood here, and that is that those isolated starfish are in some way connected to you. Thus, in saving the starfish you save yourself and everything all at the same time. There is a well-known saying in Buddhism: "From one flower you can see the whole world." Although the flower opens up in one moment, it did not just suddenly bloom. The sun, the rain, the soil, and the bees nurtured it. It too came from a seed, or a root, or a tuber that in turn came from seeds, roots, or tubers. That flower contains in it the sum of the past growth and decay of its forebears, and the germ of future seeds for generations to come. If we are to take any action on behalf of anything, we need to acknowledge that. What we eat, what we wear, what materials we consume—all were made or grown using natural resources by other individuals, transported by other individuals, transformed by chemicals or manufacturing by other individuals. Everything we have created, everything we are, is the sum of an infinite number of other acts. To honor the flower, to honor the details, is to honor everything—to bring into the hell of our lives a little bit of heaven.

8 🦎

On Sin and Buddha Nature
We Can All Become Enlightened

IN THE WEST, when we see bad things happen, we often use the notion of evil as a way to explain what happened. Either the individual or the deed itself is evil. In Buddhism, evil is in essence bad karma, and is not a static, indescribable presence—as it sometimes seems in Christianity—but, like everything else, is conditioned.

I like to think of evil in terms of water and wind. When there is no wind, water in a pond is still. However, when there is wind, the pond produces waves. But waves are not entities separate from the water; they are made of the same substance. It is only the activity of wind that turns the water from motionlessness to movement. In the same way, evil is merely a change in condition, from stillness to movement.

Because of this, bodhisattvas can retrieve even the worst offenders, even after their deaths. Likewise, everyone has the opportunity to become a Buddha, or "enlightened one." Everyone has a Buddha nature, even Osama bin Laden.

I often liken evil to fertilizer. It may stink and be unpleasant to be around, but it can allow good things to grow. The Buddha once said, "Desire is the Way." What he meant was not that we should cultivate desire. Rather he meant that we should make attempts to become aware of the desire so that we can encounter and analyze it better. The Buddha knew that we should not be afraid of desire, because we need to be able to see through it and observe that it is empty. This is why I believe it is better to bring the garbage into the open where we can deal with it, rather than keep it piling up in the basement.

For Buddhists, the nature of the condition (of the water, of our selves, etc.) is also called emptiness. There is no such thing as "the wave." The wave is the condition of water. There is no such thing as "the wind." The wind is the condition of air. There is no such thing as "water." Water is the condition of hydrogen and oxygen. There is no such thing as "air." Air is the condition of oxygen, nitrogen, and other gases. These elements are, in turn, made of molecules. These molecules are made of electrons and neutrons, and so it goes on. Yet, and here is the paradox, it takes enormous presence of mind—both literal and metaphorical—to fully understand the condition of emptiness. We need to understand the substance of things before we can understand their inherent emptiness. Once we realize that the nature of sin is fundamentally insubstantial and empty and is created by the mind, the mind is at rest and sin disappears.

To continue the elemental analogy, it is as if the Buddhist practitioner is a miner, searching for gold. She or he enters deep into the shaft and discovers the gold. The gold, however, is impure, covered in dust and rock and clustered about with other elements. In order to get to the gold, it is important to remove the layers of other elements; then, once the gold is retrieved, it is necessary to refine the gold of its impurities. This is what Buddhists mean by repentance—a washing away of impurities and refinement of the self.

After September 11, we heard the word "evil" a lot. Many Christians, including the President of the United States, have called the perpetrators of the September 11 tragedy "evil-doers." Buddhism's recognition of dependence removes the abstraction from the term and makes what we consider evil both more encompassable and more challenging. Because of the realization of interdependence, evil becomes something to which we are attached and for which we are in some way responsible. But, because we are in some way connected to that evil, it is therefore more easily conquerable than a demonic abstraction would be. Evil is thus rendered both more immediate and menacing and, paradoxically, more vulnerable.

It is as simple and as difficult as turning on a light in a dark room. All the furniture, decorations, and elements of the room were present before the light was on. But it takes illumination—and our wisdom in turning on the light—to see and appreciate them. Conversely, the darkness that we thought was so encompassing, that seemed so thick and impenetrable, the darkness that offered no hope of a way out from despair, is seen to be what it is: merely the absence of light; in itself, nothing. The darkness has not *gone* anywhere; the condition has simply changed. In a similar way, sin is only a conditioned absence of light. If we flick the switch—alter the condition—then the sin will disappear. The challenge exists in finding the switch when we are enveloped in darkness, unable to see anything, ignorant of which way to turn, groping vainly for something we know, stumbling against shapes that hurt us and feel unfamiliar to us. Changing the condition may be simple; finding our way to that understanding is hard.

9

On War and Peace
Why Do We Act Unpeacefully?

IN ONE OF my talks about September 11, a young man asked me, "Why do leaders today act unpeacefully?" It was a poignant question, one that could apply to all of us, since we often find ourselves acting out of anger and fear and bringing suffering upon someone else who we think is causing *us* suffering.

With the freedom we have in the West—and, indeed, the freedom we have as human beings—comes responsibility. This is why we should never confuse freedom with independence, even though we think that freedom *only* comes about through independence. It is thinking this way that has led to the worst forms of nationalism and racism. Such thinking encourages narrowness and isolationism, arrogance and ignorance. True freedom comes about when we recognize that we are all interdependent.

Freedom based on a false sense of independence is often a projection of ourselves onto the world. Because we are anxious about our own identities and purpose, clinging to what we believe we are, we try to control others. This is why the heart of conflict resolution is putting ourselves in someone else's shoes. Changing our position, altering our perspective, adopting a different stance—all these things can force us to rethink our own rigid positions about our identity and purpose and sense of independence. Putting ourselves in someone else's shoes is a very good way of stopping violence, whether on a personal or a national level.

We need a leadership of compassion, not a leadership of partisanship. We need a universal patriotism, not a narrow nationalism. We need to honor and defend the *patria*, or homeland, that is this planet, on which we all depend. We do not need a leadership of superpowers clashing but a leadership of compassion whose goal is world peace. Like everyone, I was shocked and sorrowful after September 11. When other such events happened around the world, people around the world and where I lived would gather together to talk about peace—but in the months immediately after the event, I found it hard to talk about peace. A friend in New York City advised me that I should not talk about peace in case I was not thought patriotic enough. I was told it would be dangerous.

Yet, in these times of interconnectivity—when we can travel around the world and communicate with people instantaneously over the telephone or the Internet, when peoples of different religious, cultural, or ethnic background live together in many countries—we need to ask ourselves, what is the meaning of the nation state and an identity solely bound up with a piece of land or an idea of nationhood?

Many young people ask me how we can persuade our leaders to adopt peaceful policies, and it is hard for me to provide an honest answer, because I am not certain that they really want to hear an opinion that is different from the answer they want. Many of us merely want to hear the things we already agree with. But Buddhism is very clear about the responsibilities and needs of peace: violence creates violence and peace creates peace. If we only look narrowly at a situation, then we will fail to make a difference; the more widely and deeply we look, the greater our forethought and genuine consideration of others, the more successful will be our action.

Once we realize that our efforts to project who we are, and what we believe, onto the world are futile, we stop expecting, or even desiring others to be like us. I think that the global dynamics between al-Qaeda and the Western powers reveal this particular dynamic very sharply. Each has an idea of what they think is best, projecting their ideas on to the other. The result is tragedy. When we stop expecting and desiring others to be like us there is less resistance, less confusion, and less confrontation. It is important to remember that Buddhism has the distinction of being the only major world religion that has never engaged in holy wars. Could it be otherwise for a belief system that has written in its scriptures, "Buddhism is in the midst of respectfulness"?

The life of the ancient Buddhist king Asoka is a great example of the relationship between respect and a prosperous community. The conversion of King Asoka to Buddhism ushered in an age of splendor in India. As a result of his conversion, he refrained from killing, reduced taxes, and respected all religions. His subjects loved him, and the nation grew prosperous and strong. As Master Hsing Yun points out about Asoka's kingdom, "Tolerating differences will not lead to division. It will only increase vitality and bring in fullness and blossoming." The five fingers of the hand are different from one another; some are long and some are shorter. Together, they can work miracles. This is the message that all leaders need to understand—and, if we are to become true leaders like Asoka, the rest of us need to understand it, too.

These ideas can be applied not only to the individual and his sense of self, but to all such categories understood by the human mind—even religion itself.

Buddhism allows us liberation from the attachment to permanence by freeing us from what can seem to be the impossibility of change and, potentially, from the disappointments that belief in permanence constantly creates for us. Our conditionality, our full interdependence with each other and the world around us, can allow us to relate our suffering to that of other living beings by making their suffering our own. But it can also make us aware that our own suffering is merely a condition that can be alleviated by recognizing that that feeling, too, can change.

Buddhism is not about the denial of the self. It is not about withdrawing from the world. On the contrary, we can all change the world. But we need to know that we change *with* the world, and that that "we" is constantly changing *in* the world. This is true leadership.

10 ☙
On Compassion and Wisdom
What the World Needs Now

B UDDHISM SAYS THAT compassion is generated by seeing that everything is interrelated. If my finger is hurt, it affects how I behave. If I knock my hand, I will feel uncomfortable. I might not be able to work. I might have a headache. The suffering I am experiencing is not localized merely to my finger—even though it might be advisable to deal with the localized problem. In a similar way, I can recognize that a Chinese woman may feel anger and resentment against what happened to her during the Cultural Revolution. She is a victim. She is a victim in the same way that the Tibetans are victims.

Yet even murderers and perpetrators of injustice are victims, in that they suffer because their minds are polluted.

The conditions that surround them lead them to make wrong judgments. I realize that this is very controversial, but I think the hijackers of the planes were victims of their blind faith and biased judgment. They need our compassion, too.

If we want to get to the meaning of the idea of compassion in Buddhism, it is necessary to understand interdependence or coexistence. Compassion means extending yourself into the mind of the person who has done you or others harm and recognizing that that person is conditioned by his or her background. The World Trade Center bombers were not born to kill people. But they might have been led to do that terrible act because they felt their world was threatened by the West, or they were misled by a blind faith that failed to acknowledge the suffering of others. When we try and profile a World Trade Center bomber, we recognize that he was conditioned and that everybody in one way or another contributed to that conditioning. Those bombers were loved, had families who cared about them: their families also deserve our compassion.

It is very important to emphasize that this understanding of conditioning should not be used as an excuse to avoid responsibility. Buddhism does not deny individual responsibility. The Buddhist insights that we are all conditioned, that the self is dependent, and that all is impermanent, do not mean that the perpetrator can claim that, since everything is conditioned and coexistent, he does not bear any responsibility for his actions. As I suggested in my chapter on karma, all actions—whether good or bad—produce karma; and karma is not only collective, it is also individual. While we are not totally free in our actions, we are not totally dependent, either.

Like Christianity, Buddhism understands that human beings have free will. Because we are interdependent, however, Buddhism places free will within the context of the interdependence of other beings. In seeking to understand the nature of the mind and suffering, Buddhists attempt to discover the purer part of themselves. This attempt on the part of free will is to make the will to be good that much stronger. Through disciplines such as meditation, the Buddhist seeks to make judgments about existence that are less skewed by bias or clouded with impure thoughts or conceptions. The task of the Buddhist practitioner is to peel away the layers of illusion that cloud our judgment. This great task is accomplished by the exercise of free will; in turn, it enlarges the power and purity of the will. Unlike Christianity, Buddhism does not see free will as a gift from God. Like everything else, free will is conditioned. This places even more emphasis on us to exercise our free will responsibly—to do more good than bad.

If we understand that sin is emptiness, that it is a function of the conditioned mind, we are able to get to the heart of the other essential Buddhist tenet: compassion. Sin is empty because it is conditioned, and the conditions that create sin are conditions that we all share. In Buddhism, everything is connected. Nothing can be simply explained by looking at isolated pieces of existence. You have to look at the whole.

Such holistic thinking can sometimes seem very alien to Western thinkers, raised with the idea of the autonomous individual with a self. Sometimes people say to me that they do not believe in the concept that behind the self there is emptiness, because, they add, if they hit me or cut me with a knife I would feel pain. The way I respond is to say that of course there is a self, but, like everything else, it is conditioned; it exists not as an isolated entity but in connection with everything else.

Buddhism, to repeat, does not absolve people of their actions because of claims there is no self that is doing the action or that, because we are interdependent, there is no perpetrator or victim. Buddhism binds all our deeds together so that every deed—no matter how trivial—is consequential. Thus action of any sort needs to be the well-considered offshoot of a pure mind, if the consequences are to be good for yourself, let alone anyone or anything else. This is how compassion is bound up with wisdom.

Compassion generates wisdom because it allows you to move beyond the merely sensuous understanding of the world to insight and perception. Wisdom requires attentiveness. It is like being handed a glass full of murky water, shaken constantly by our karmic activities. First, we need to let the glass stop shaking and the water become motionless. Then, slowly, the dust particles will begin to sink to the bottom of the glass and the water will begin to clear. The sediment does not disappear. It is merely more clearly seen. Likewise, suffering and evil—all those conditions that cloud our clear perception—do not disappear. They become more visible, and thus more easily contained.

Our challenge as Buddhists is to let the water become still. In Buddhism, we have a saying: If a pond is murky, it is hard to see the moon. I would add that, even worse than that, if a pond is murky, and you are creating waves, then the moon is not only hard to see, but the moon's shape—when it is glimpsed—is distorted. The only thing worse than not being able to see clearly is to think you are seeing something clearly when you are not.

I remember visiting a cave in Virginia with some friends. At the very bottom of the tunnel there was an underground lake with water so clear that it was almost impossible to see the water. Only if you touched this unpolluted water did you see the shimmering of the clear liquid. Likewise, in Buddhism, if the mind is clear then it is possible to reflect things as they are, without distortion or without a distance between you and the thing reflected upon. But this can only come about when there is stillness and we stop shaking things up.

This is why Buddhism teaches us not to rush to judgment about people. We are always making judgments about people and things, and they are often wrong. Not only are they inaccurate—outpourings of our own anxieties, fears, prejudices, and ignorance—but they are usually founded on pieces rather than the whole. One day you may like your partner; the next day he or she may drive you crazy. Everywhere we look we are given signals by society about who is good and who is bad, what is heroic and what is not. It is a simplistic, one-sided view of things that only perpetuates a distorted view of reality. Life is not like that: the good and the bad do not always do good or bad things.

In Buddhism, there is no such thing as good and bad people; there are only good or bad deeds. Thinking this way means that we cannot set the "evil-doer" outside of our own life and say that he or she has nothing to do with us. It means that we cannot say that we bear no responsibility for his or her actions. It means that we cannot say that that person is possessed by something we could never be possessed by. It means that have to examine our own lives, our own bad deeds, our own responsibility for generating bad karma. It means we have to examine whether we, too, think thoughts that could generate harm. We cannot escape our responsibility.

This is why the search for wisdom within Buddhism is so hard. It is relentlessly honest. Truly Buddhist thought does not settle on a point and say that every problem has been solved. Every moment is filled with the possibility of good and bad actions because we are conditioned, interdependent, and impermanent. Wisdom means recognizing those conditions and becoming clear-minded about them.

Part Two
Personal Suffering

11 ✺
On Suffering
Our Common Experience

FOR SIDDHARTHA GAUTAMA, the Buddha, the nature of suffering was the essential question facing all human beings. Suffering afflicted rich and poor, the powerful and the powerless, men and women. How the Buddha came to understand this is the foundational story of the Buddhist religion.

As a young man, the Buddha lived in luxury as a prince of the realm, confined by his father Suddhodana in a palace in northern India and surrounded by riches and pleasurable diversions. One day, however, while riding in his coach through the city, Siddhartha glanced out of the window and saw an old man, hunched over, leaning on a cane, making his way home. Questioning his charioteer as to what was wrong with the man, the young prince was told that the man was merely old, a condition that comes to us all. On another day, the prince saw a man who appeared very sick. The man's condition was confirmed by the charioteer, who explained that we too are all subject to sickness. On yet another journey, the prince saw a dead body, and the charioteer reminded him that we all must die. Finally, the Buddha saw a man robed in yellow with no hair on his head and was told this was a *sanyasin,* an ascetic who had renounced the wealth of the world and wandered through it seeking serenity.

The young went home to the palace, shaved his head, and became a *sanyasin,* leaving behind his wife and child and ceding them all his possessions. He visited many teachers and practiced many disciplines, including extreme asceticism. Finding that such asceticism had not brought him to the Truth, the renunciate rested underneath a bodhi tree and, sitting cross-legged, decided that he would not get up until he had achieved Enlightenment. After being tormented by the demon, Mara—who attempted to distract him with false hopes and desires—Siddhartha Gautama achieved enlightenment, and became the Enlightened One, or Buddha.

The consequences of the Buddha's enlightenment were his realization of the Four Noble Truths. Theses truths form the core of Buddhist teachings. They are, first, that all existence is suffering; secondly, that this suffering has a cause; thirdly, that suffering can be overcome; and, fourthly, that there is a way to bring about the end of suffering. In contemplating how to bring about release from suffering, the Buddha realized the Eightfold Path. These principles are: right understanding, right thought, right speech, right action, right livelihood, right effort, right mindfulness, and right concentration. In sum, these principles are as follows: Once we understand the causes of suffering and cultivate action based on correct thinking and thoughtful speech, if we also live correctly and with mindfulness and using meditation, then the path is open to overcome the suffering inherent in being alive.

Buddhism, therefore, is a very practical religion. It is concerned with finding solutions to pressing needs. Already as a young man in his chariot, the Buddha saw how our life is full of suffering—sickness, old age, and death—and he was shocked by it. What the wealthy, sheltered, naïve young man realized is that these central events in our life were not abstractions or the experience of only the poor; they were inevitable and came to everyone, even to this wealthy, handsome prince who had it all. The central purpose of the Buddha's life then became trying to find a way to understand and then overcome suffering.

The Buddha's journey encompassed two key components that should be understood when thinking of our own spiritual paths. First, he moved from the utmost luxury to the utmost deprivation, and then realized that neither of them helped. This is why Buddhism is called the Middle Way—and why it is skeptical of the claims of truth, revelation, or knowledge that come from extremes. The second is that the Buddha's aim was not merely personal salvation, nor even the salvation of all other people, but the salvation of all sentient beings.

While Buddhism is, as I have said, very practical, at its center it also places emphasis on right understanding and right thinking. According to Buddhist thought, therefore, before there can be right action, there has to be right thought, and right thought depends on a correct analysis of the conditions of your own life and existence in general. This is why in order to understand suffering, it is necessary to understand the nature of the mind and the nature of the self. Buddhism's insights into consciousness and the mind and the self are one of its great gifts to humankind. In the next chapters I shall explore the different modes of suffering and the nature of the mind and the self.

12 ❦
The Eight Kinds of Suffering
Suffering from the Outside and the Inside

IN BUDDHISM, THERE are different kinds of suffering that are compartmentalized in different ways to emphasize different aspects of suffering. In some Buddhist traditions, suffering is divided in two ways. One type of suffering is that which comes from outside us—for example, natural disasters, accidents, disease, and such outrages as the World Trade Center attack. The other type is the suffering that is generated from inside us. This suffering might be a sense of dissatisfaction when, for instance, we want more than we have been given or we are not happy with who we are. This is a basic division.

Buddhism splits suffering into eight different categories. This chapter will spend some time with each type of suffering, since each bears directly on our daily lives and, I believe, offers some insight into how we can reframe the problems that suffering creates.

The First Kind of Suffering

The first kind of suffering is caused by birth. People often see birth as a joyful event—the bringing of new life into the world, the experience of parenthood, the feeling that one's family will continue beyond one's own death. All of these experiences are, indeed, potentially full of joy, and are to be honored. Nevertheless, birth is also attended by a great deal of suffering. In many countries around the world the act of giving birth is surrounded by great pain and also a substantial amount of mortality—many babies and mothers die in childbirth because they do not have access to hygiene or sterile implements, or there may be complications in the position of the fetus or in the mother's loss of blood. Even if the birth is free of complication and there are midwives and doctors in attendance, the experience of giving birth is excruciatingly painful—so much so that Western medicine has created drugs such as epidural injections to numb the body. No matter how numb we become, however, that numbness should tell us something about the life we are entering into and how much pain we will experience and wish to avoid.

In addition to childbirth itself there is the fact that the baby him- or herself is moving from the womb, where it has been in a comfortable, sealed environment, into a new world that is different and strange. This is why the baby cries. Even though it may be good for a baby to exercise its lungs as soon as it is born, that she or he does so by crying rather than laughing somehow points to a primal recognition of suffering that Buddhism makes the First Noble Truth.

In April 2000, I was invited by UNICEF to participate in their Safe Motherhood Project. I was there as a consultant to help attendees understand why, from a cultural standpoint, the rate of maternal mortality in South Asia was so high in comparison with the maternal mortality rate of Europe. I suggested that some of the cultural reasons for such a situation might be that people thought the blood was impure and that women were not valuable. This meant that when women gave birth they reacted extremely negatively to all the blood, or the husbands of the women in childbirth would rather their wife die and have another wife, with another dowry. It may seem incredible to hear that anyone could feel this way in the twenty-first century, but this situation is not unusual in some countries in South Asia. Even people working in the hospitals can be alarmingly indifferent to the rights of women and children, which leads to many deaths. When the very first stages of life are greeted with such indifference or even hostility, how can we deny the presence of suffering in birth?

It has always been the case, and it remains so today, that the lives of children are deeply threatened and vulnerable. Children have always relied on adults to provide them with food and care, yet more and more it seems children are under threat. They are physically, sexually, or emotionally abused; they are abandoned in dumpsters or left to fend for themselves on the streets. They are sold into slavery (as they are in Sudan), the sex trade (for instance, in Thailand and Cambodia), forced to become thieves or, even worse, soldiers (such as in Sierra Leone), or kidnapped and trained to be suicide bombers, as is the case with the Tamil Tigers in Sri Lanka. They suffer from malnutrition or from obesity; they are deprived of the simplest staples in their lives and bombarded with products to make them feel inadequate. From the richest mansions of the United States to the poorest back streets of India, children are increasingly on their own. And, as recent reports have made clear, children—along with their mothers—constitute by far the majority of the world's poor.

How does Buddhism look at the phenomenon of the suffering of birth and childhood? In Chinese Buddhism, there is no such thing as a birthday. Instead of calling it a "birthday" we call it "the day our mother suffered"—a way of reminding us that suffering attends our existence from our first moments, and that it is a suffering somehow shared between mother and child. A birthday is, thus, considered a day to reflect with gratitude on the sacrifices our mother has made for us.

In this way, Buddhism seeks to examine our tendency toward sentimentality and closed-heartedness when it comes to the lives of children other than our own and advocates a compassion based on the experience of all children. It demands that we be responsible for them, and recognize that their lives are precious and their fears genuine, no matter the circumstances in which they are born. When we think this way, we should see it as our responsibility that forty million children around the world have AIDS, or that many millions of children face daily starvation in Afghanistan and all around the world. They are our children, too.

I should make clear here that when Buddhism in the First Noble Truth talks about all life being suffering, it does not necessarily mean that, even though we enter this world in shock and in suffering, we have to *end* our life in suffering. Indeed, Buddhism is about diminishing or neutralizing the suffering that is inherent in life's passages and achieving happiness.

The Second Kind of Suffering

The second kind of suffering has to do with aging, one of the sufferings of course that Siddhartha Gautama came upon when riding in his chariot. It should be obvious why aging is associated with suffering. We find it harder to walk and do the things we used to do. We get tired more easily, and men worry about losing their hair and women about having more wrinkles. Our minds may forget things and, as happens to some unfortunate people, suffer from some form of dementia. For those whose minds remain strong and alert, it is an exquisite feature of the suffering of aging that we conceive of ourselves as young and vital while our bodies tell us we are otherwise.

Of course, there are great gifts in growing older: we have wisdom and experience, we have garnered some respect from society and achieved a position in the world. But the aging process, unfortunately, does not take that into consideration or pause to pay its respects to our wisdom! Nor does aging hold itself back because we have achieved something within society. Clearly, there is suffering in aging.

The Third Kind of Suffering
The third category of suffering in Buddhism is sickness and disease. Sickness and disease are not only physical but can also be mental—all involve suffering, even though the suffering may vary in scope or degree. The categories of physical and mental suffering also encompass not only the ailments of cancer, diabetes, and other types of physical diseases, or dementia, Alzheimer's, and other sorts of mental diseases. They also encompass the psychological pain that is involved when we are debilitated by disease—such as when paraplegics or quadriplegics are unable to move their bodies as their mind wishes, or when people who have suffered strokes cannot move one side of their body. As with the previous kind of suffering, such suffering is about the inability to do the things we once could, even though our mind is sharp and wants us to be able to move.

The suffering of illness also encompasses the loss of dignity, such as when the body does things we do not want it to do—when we are incontinent or have nervous tics, or when the synapses and nerve endings send incorrect signals to the brain. In such a situation, the physical suffering we are undergoing is compounded by our embarrassment and our fear of dependency.

The Fourth Kind of Suffering

The fourth category is death. Death is not only the suffering we are ourselves undergoing as we die but also the suffering of the people around us who love us and do not want to see us go. Buddhism describes death as a time when our soul leaves the body and compares it to a turtle leaving its shell or a snake shedding its skin. Buddhists believe that it is painful for the soul to leave the body—irrespective of whether our death is attended by injury, disease, or physical pain—because our physical body is that to which we are most obviously attached. As such, our karmic bond to it is that much greater.

The Fifth Kind of Suffering

The fifth category is the suffering of departing from the people we love. This suffering occurs not only when we die. For instance, we might have recently got married and then had to go to work or somewhere else, leaving our loved one behind. This kind of suffering is particularly subtle, because not only is there the suffering of leaving someone behind, but there is the suffering of knowing when we are with them that the time will come when we must leave them again. So we suffer when we are away from them, and we suffer when we are with them in the knowledge that we will have to depart from each other sometime. This kind of suffering challenges in a very intense way our attachment to loved ones by forcing us to acknowledge our dependence on them and, indeed, our interdependence with them.

The Sixth Kind of Suffering

The sixth kind of suffering is one that amuses many people who are new to Buddhism. It is the suffering of being with somebody we hate. We may have a colleague whom we dislike intensely, but our job makes it necessary for us to work with this person, or our boss requires it. In fact, is it not the case that we find ourselves spending as much time with the colleague we dislike as we do with the loved one we miss so much? Sometimes we may feel it is even more! This suffering only enhances our feelings of suffering at not being with the one we want to be with while increasing our resentment at being with the one we hate.

What both the fifth and sixth kinds of suffering point to is that our human relationships are fraught with false expectations and needless confrontations. It is not too much to say that all the problems we suffer from in relationships come down to attachment. Many of us enter relationships—whether intimate or otherwise—believing that we need to have a partner for us to have self-esteem. My students often feel they need to have a boyfriend or a girlfriend in order to feel good about themselves. Or businesspeople may feel that they have to be respected and revered by their workers or their clients in order to feel they are successful or powerful.

What these experiences come down to is that many of us feel that unless we are loved and recognized by another person we are not worth anything. As far as dealing with day-to-day suffering, I think it is very important that we love and recognize our own worth from inside us, so that no matter whether anybody loves us or not, no matter whether our loved one leaves us for someone else or is torn away from us in a disaster or through an illness, we know for ourselves that we are good, and that their departure is not necessarily our fault or a consequence of our behavior.

Some people might say that by saying we need to value ourselves I am abandoning our recognition of conditionality in favor of individualism. Not so. What I am saying, to the contrary, is that if we recognize our self-worth we become more lovable because we are in turn more generous to others. Confidence in the self is a confidence that has a potential to give more because it comes from a sounder foundation. Clearly, arrogance and pride are states of mind whereby the self has forgotten its conditionality in favor of self-aggrandizement. Karma will probably dictate that the arrogant and proud individual will be brought down through his or her own actions. Nevertheless, Buddhism agrees with the human potential movement in calling for a centered self that can give so much to the world because it does not need to take so much to survive.

Both the fifth and sixth forms of suffering concern our relationships—and this is one of the other major causes of suffering. I am struck by the fact that many people look for quantity rather than quality in their intimate relationships, focusing on pleasure and desire rather than happiness. My students in Taiwan surprise me when they tell me they are actively looking to have one-night stands. While having sex may be harmless if all the precautions about sexually transmitted diseases are taken, we simply do not know how others will be affected by such behavior. As French philosopher and theologian Blaise Pascal (1623–1662) once said, "The heart has its reasons of which reason knows nothing," and the consequences of our having a one-night stand with someone might lead the person with whom you had sex to become emotionally attached and fall in love with you. She or he might become hurt by your subsequent indifference. You yourself might fall in love and be hurt in turn.

Once more, we have to acknowledge the laws of cause and effect. Our sexuality is a powerful signal of who we are and triggers all kinds of emotions. Being casual about it will be sure to bring consequences, and we should be prepared to respond to them. We need to ask ourselves what we truly want from our relationships, and it seems to me that really we should want to have no relationships at all rather than ones that are bad or self-destructive.

The consequences of our sexual behavior and our sense of the need to be loved can be positive. But they can also be very negative. For instance, I have been stunned at the amount of domestic violence there is in the West, and in the United States in particular—violence that cuts across class and race. Clearly, there is great trauma and suffering associated with the need to acquire and control in our relationships. It is as if we are trying to find out about ourselves or express ourselves, but we are doing it in the wrong way. We are attaching our self-worth to money or power or status and trying to prove we are a better person because we have a better job, or a prettier wife, or a faster car. We somehow believe that acquisition means happiness, even though the real person—the one behind the big suit or the high-walled mansion, or inside the stretch limo—has the same needs as the poorest, least influential person in society. Essentially, we have forgotten not only our needs but who we are. When, in some way, we realize that none of these things makes us happy, we seem to lash out at whoever is near us.

We need to go back to ourselves and ask ourselves those questions: Who are we? What do we really want? Why are we on this planet? If we can access our inner wealth, the enormous treasures that we have inside us, then we will never be poor or unimportant. Buddhism has a saying that reflects this knowledge. We each may be like a poor child who has millions of pearls in his or her pocket but does not know what they are or how to use them. Our wealth is right there with us. We simply need to be able to recognize it and use it properly.

The richness of inner wealth balances the poverty of external wealth. The more we have inside, the less we will need to have on the outside to buttress our sense of inner worth. Possessions then become things we can give away or use to the benefit of all beings rather than ways to make us feel good about ourselves. The person with inner wealth does not need to prove how important or intelligent or wealthy he or she is. Likewise, people with inner poverty will always be showing us how much they have. They may not be equal in material terms, but Buddhism believes that everyone is equal in inner treasure.

The Seventh Kind of Suffering

The seventh category of suffering is one that was touched upon when I mentioned the two types of suffering; it is the suffering that comes from not having things we want. We may want to be the president of the company but we do not get chosen, or we want to be a politician but we do not get voted in, or we may want to have a car but we cannot acquire one, or we are addicted to drugs and we cannot get an extra supply. Likewise, we may love someone who does not love us. This is one of the most common forms of suffering, and it is caused by craving and attachment.

Many people in the West have two major misconceptions about Buddhism. The first one is that Buddhism believes it is wrong to have possessions. The second is that Buddhism believes that everything you have should be unadorned. As to the second misconception: Buddhism does not want everything to be simple and plain. Buddhism responds to beauty, to luxury, vibrant colors, skill, and artifice. I always encourage people to respect beauty and craftsmanship. I see craftsmanship and even mechanical sophistication as artistic expressions. For instance, a really beautiful car or a highly crafted watch is to be admired for its expressiveness as well as its mechanical complexity. Buddhism is not about blandness.

What Buddhism asks us to do—and this relates to the first misconception—is to keep remembering that everything is interdependent. Thus, for instance, if we drive a very expensive car but it has a very inefficient or polluting engine, then we need to acknowledge our responsibility in polluting the planet and consuming natural resources that might be used by other beings. The car itself—the chassis, the stylings, the artistry of the interior—might not be the problem; the engine and its consumption is. Buddhism asks us to make differentiations between the utility of an object and its beauty. Beauty does not consume. Therefore, possessions in and of themselves are not bad for Buddhists, even monks or nuns. While it is important to lead a simple life and follow the middle path, it is what we *do* with what we have rather than *what* we have that matters. Buddhism responds and respects variety—we are not all the same, nor should we be. But when we affect the lives of other beings and the planet, then we need to have restraint and discipline.

This is why I feel strongly that cathedrals and temples have a role in fostering feelings of the divine. Some people feel that building temples or churches is a waste of money. But I think the difference between a small hut and visiting the Vatican or a great temple is that the magnitude expresses the divine. There is more awe, more reverence, as well as beauty. I would not want all society to stagnate in sameness or frugality for the sake of frugality. But there needs to be restraint. For instance, I love ivory, but I do not think it is suitable to cause pain to animals by killing elephants to get it.

This is how Buddhism responds to the phenomenon of consumption and makes its accommodation with capitalism. Buddhism believes in the freedom of the individual to achieve his or her own goals, to follow his or her own mission in this world. The Buddha's choice of the Middle Way was at least partly brought about by his recognition that asceticism merely for its own sake was not bringing him any nearer to enlightenment than was luxury for its own sake. But Buddhism is mindful—and I use the word deliberately—of the suffering that is latent when we consume natural resources or the products of natural resources. In the case of ivory above, I have decided that, on consideration and based on the facts as I understand them, my pleasure at the craftsmanship and beauty of the product made with ivory was not worth the suffering of the living being that had to experience pain to have the ivory removed. This is not a matter of utilitarian balancing between relative suffering. Buddhism sees our judgments as threads connected through time to all existence. In deciding what to do in a given situation, our behavior is not merely juggling consequences as they occur to us, but living our lives fully in the recognition that everything we do has causes and consequences.

As a Buddhist, therefore, I try to reflect simplicity and beauty in everything I do. I respond to variety and artistry even as I practice my disciplines and pare down the inessentials. This is not a paradox, but more an interplay that is intrinsically Buddhist, because, to paraphrase *Hamlet,* there is nothing either good or bad but action makes it so, and everything can be made beautiful or ugly by what we decide to do with it.

Becoming aware of the attachment we have to possessions and money is hard. There is a story of a man who lived very meagerly but had a pile of gold bars, which he wrapped in newspaper and hid under his bed. People who lived near the man knew he was rich but never saw him use any of his gold. One day, thieves broke into his house and stole all his gold and the man was heartbroken. "Since you never use the gold," the man's neighbors said, "why do not you take some bricks and wrap them in newspaper and then put them under your bed? What's the difference?"

I like this story because I think too many of us do not make our money valuable, we just like to see the numbers getting bigger in the bank. There is another Buddhist saying that points out that even though we may have a thousand acres, every night we only need about six feet for sleep. And even though we have a hundred dishes for our food, we can only eat as much as will fill us up. So we need to enjoy the things we have and know our limits at the same time. We also need to acknowledge our appetites—acquisitiveness, greed—and our attachment to them. Only by doing that will we be able to unattach ourselves from them and save ourselves and others much suffering.

What I tell my students is that we need to be selective in what we decide to take from life, because we are surrounded by junk—junk food, junk mail, junk relationships, junk emotions, and junk thoughts. Junk is attractive because it can seem enticing and might even feel or taste good to start off with. Indeed, it is designed to be most attractive to us by appealing to our appetites and appetitiveness, our needs and urges. But we know beforehand, and we sure know afterward, that junk is not good for us. In a junk world, our desire for junk is never satisfied, except when we have consumed so much of it that we are sickened by it. It sets off all sorts of craving in us, and we need to be careful around it. This means discipline and restraint. Our thoughts are like oxen running around in a field. We need to watch them so they do not run wild. We need to discipline our mind and desire.

The Eighth Kind of Suffering

The eighth kind of suffering is, in many ways, a summation of all the suffering caused by our five aggregates—all the elements of our physical and mental make-up as well as sensation, conception, volition, and consciousness. We suffer physically and psychologically. We may be hungry and not have enough food, or we are thirsty and do not have enough water, or we need shelter but we are homeless. As Daoist philosopher Laozi says, "Our great suffering is because we have this body." Because of this body we experience aging, sickness, and death, and in our mind we also experience suffering because we are forced to see the change our body is undergoing.

Now, some might say, having discussed all the different modes of suffering I have listed above, that the world and their lives are not always characterized by suffering. And in this they may be correct—because we *do* know joy, and there are moments when that experience is not just ours, or our family's, or even our nation's. The fall of the Berlin Wall was an event that unleashed a great deal of happiness across the entire continent of Europe.

However, even joyful or happy sensations can bring about suffering, because they too will not last forever. Once more, we have to take into account the impermanence of all things. Furthermore, suffering is also created by the change from happiness to unhappiness and back again. At times, we may feel neither happy nor sad, but neutral. Everything is in flux between states. I remember sitting on the subway train from Queens as it moved toward Manhattan and I began to look at the skyline and search for the Twin Towers, as I had done many times. And I could not find them. In my mind they were still there, and in reality they were not. The recognition of impermanence and flux is its own kind of suffering.

All these modes of suffering are caused by desire, hatred, or ignorance. Desire reflects on when we want to have more or be with someone more. Hatred obviously refers to those we hate but who are present with us; and illusion or ignorance is about how we do not expect impermanence in our mind but it constantly comes back to us. And these three are connected: Desire creates attachment, and craving creates hatred, and ignorance creates all of them. All depend on a failure to perceive the true nature of the self, which is what I will discuss next.

13 ❦
On the Self and Suffering
Who Suffers?

W E TALK ABOUT ourselves a lot; we also talk about our *selves* a lot. But what exactly is the self? And how is it possible to talk about it? Certainly, we can talk about our achievements and actions. But am I simply the combination of everything I have done in my life? Is that really *who* I am?

In my second year of high school, I was too busy with student activities to be a good student and fell from being top in my class to fifty-sixth. For someone with as strong an ethic of work and study as myself, it was a huge shock. I did not know whether I was really the first person and had sunk to fifty-sixth, or actually the fifty-sixth person who had miraculously been first for a while. Even though it was hard to unattach myself from *feeling* belittled or aggrieved at my lowly status, that was the first inkling I had that where I was ranked had nothing to do with *me*; it was all about the effort and time I put in. I wish I could say I became much less competitive. However, I was just as anxious and competitive when I undertook my Ph.D.!

We find it very hard not to define ourselves by our achievements. You might be a movie star who, by the time you are seventeen years old, has earned enough money to buy a house in Beverly Hills. When you are nineteen, however, you have lost all your money. You do not know whether you are the rich boy who lost lots of money or the poor boy who suddenly and temporarily became rich. This situation happens to many of us all the time. If we are laid off from work, are we someone who once belonged to a company and got fired, or were we someone who happened to work for that company for a short period of time? Are we still the manager we used to be or someone who thought we were a manager but weren't? Are we the unfortunate boss or lucky worker? Where is the real *I*—the true, unchanging, absolute *I*?

This is what I tell my students. I tell them that there is nothing wrong with money or prestige or even power, but that we need to ask ourselves constantly: Am I happy with myself? Am I in control of myself? We should ask ourselves these questions before we set out on the road to wealth, prestige, and power. Then, should we achieve any or all of these things, we should ask the questions again. And when or if we lose any or all of these things or even become the reverse— poor, notorious, or powerless—we should ask ourselves the questions yet again. If, in all these three stages, we can know ourselves and manage ourselves, then we can do anything we set our heart on.

These examples show an obvious truth—one that the Buddha discovered after he returned to the palace and decided to become a renunciate: it is foolish to try and establish our identities, or seek happiness, solely through our social status. It will not protect us from suffering and it will never fully satisfy us. Many try to run away from who we are, and cling to status as our identity. This is wrong. We are not the sum of how successful or unsuccessful we are in this life. We are not what other people think we are, or should be; and we should not judge ourselves by other people's impressions of us.

The Body

The second truth that comes from the Buddha's realizations is that the physical body changes. The young prince Siddhartha gauged his own youthful beauty against the sick man and the old man and realized that his body would change just as those two individuals' bodies had changed. Yet we often feel our body is the most permanent thing we know. For instance, we look at ourselves in the mirror and there we are. We recognize ourselves. We are permanent. Indeed, we all know who we are. We are Peter or Mary and we are here, and, as if to confirm the solidity of our presence, people respond to us as though we were here as well.

But this permanence is an illusion. After all, we weren't always what we are now; we had a very different shape and identity when we were babies, or adolescents. We have all had those experiences of coming across a friend whom we have not seen for many years and being unable to recognize him until he told us who he was. The question remains: Even though he looks completely different, is he still the same Michael whom we knew all those years ago?

There is a ghost story that illustrates what I mean by these two truths. There was once a man, whom we will call Mr. Johnson, who one night entered an abandoned house and discovered a dead body. Later on, he saw two ghosts entering the house. The first ghost saw the corpse and wanted to eat it; but the second ghost told the first that the corpse belonged to him, because he had seen it first. The second ghost was larger, however, and tried to bully the first. While they were arguing, they glimpsed Mr. Johnson hiding in the corner. Unable to resolve their argument, the ghosts asked the terrified man to come over and judge who should eat the body. Because he had seen the first ghost entering the house first, Mr. Johnson said that the dead body belonged to the first ghost. At this, the second ghost was so angry that he ripped off Mr. Johnson's arm and ate it. Immediately, the first ghost ripped an arm from the corpse and attached it to Mr. Johnson's body.

The second ghost then took another arm from Mr. Johnson and the first ghost attached the other arm from the corpse to Mr. Johnson's body. Part by part, the ghosts replaced Mr. Johnson's body with the dead one, leaving Mr. Johnson to wonder who he was. Was he still Mr. Johnson?

While this story seems absurd, contemporary scientific endeavors are making it into a distinct possibility. Organ transplants are becoming routine. What if our arms, kidneys, and hearts are artificial or transplanted from someone else? What happens if a majority, perhaps eighty percent, of our body has been changed? Are we still then who we were? Could we then claim that the physical body we see in the mirror is who we are? If our body changes as we age, and if our body changes because other bodies or body parts now make up our body, can we determine who or what that absolute self is that we think is *who* we are?

The Possible Locations of the Self

The quest for what it is precisely that makes us distinctly ourselves, the part of us that never changes, has perplexed and challenged philosophers for centuries. Some people say that it is not in the body that the self resides, but in the feelings we have. We know who we are because we feel it. But, as we all have experienced many times, feelings are very unreliable signposts of who we are. We get hot and we get cold. We may get up in the morning feeling sad; a good breakfast may make us feel happy; and then we get in our car and drive to work and hit a traffic jam and get angry. We are back to feeling sad again.

To those who would argue that it is the simple fact that we *do* feel that makes us who we are, rather than particular feelings at any one time, I would argue that we should examine the nature of that feeling about feelings! How do we know that that feeling is not itself subject to change? The trouble with feelings is that they are so emotional! They *always* change. It seems to me to be obvious that, because we can feel so many emotions, locating the self within the emotions is not going to work.

The French philosopher and mathematician René Descartes (1596–1650) famously said: "I think, therefore I am." Because of this, some people place the self in our capacity to think and in our thoughts. However, our thoughts are even more changeable than our feelings. Part of the point of meditation, Buddhism recognizes, is to still the mind and somehow stop the plethora of thoughts that constantly arise and pass through our minds. After all, we are constantly changing our minds, thinking new things, acting impulsively without thinking things through, being thoughtless. How many relationships have been broken off or restarted because someone changed their mind? If the mind really is where our self resides, then all we can say is that the self is changeable.

Some people consider the memory to be the proper location of self. After all, our memories are carried across time— as the body changes, as our thoughts change, as our feelings change, our memories, so it is argued, are always with us, and thus remain where our identity is. But, then, how are we to account for people who lose their memory—whether permanently or temporarily? If we suffer from a temporary memory loss, does that mean we cease to be who we are? When a loved one gets Alzheimer's disease, some caregivers feel their loved ones are no longer the person they were, while others feel they are. Is it really the case that when we lose our memory our identity is lost as well?

There was a British conductor and broadcaster who specialized in the complex music of the Renaissance, by the name of Clive Wearing. In the mid-1980s, Mr. Wearing became infected by encephalitis, which destroyed much of the hippocampus and frontal lobe areas of the brain. These are the places that scientists believe house our short-term memory. Thus, while Mr. Wearing was able to carry on normal long-term memory functions—such as walking, talking, writing, even playing and conducting music—whenever anybody stopped him and asked him what he was doing, he could not remember. More terrifying for him was that he did not know who he was. Indeed, every twenty minutes or so when he wasn't engaged in playing music or some such long-term activity, Mr. Wearing would suddenly come to life and feel his personal identity. He would write that he felt alive for the first time. Yet, after a few moments of consciousness, he would forget who he was. Every time the musician "awoke" to his new identity, he would read what he had written the previous time and be unable to remember when he wrote it or how he felt when he wrote it. He even had no idea of who he was when he wrote it. So he would be even more emphatic in writing a statement that he was alive. Each time he "awoke," it felt new.

Even twenty years after the onset of the infection, Mr. Wearing is still unable to hold a consciousness over any length of time, even though he now has some fragmentary grasp of what has happened to him and what will occur to him when he lapses into "unconsciousness." He does, however, have a feeling about his life. It is a life without dreams or thoughts. For him there is no difference between day and night, between the day before and the day to come. Neither sight nor sound means anything to him because there is nothing to compare them with or use them for. Twenty years later, he says, it still feels "just like death."

Certainly, this musician's identity is tied up with his memory. Ironically, when he was not himself the musician was most recognizable to those who had known him before his illness: he performed and read music and in every way seemed to be in control of his surroundings. Yet, when he was stopped in the middle of conducting, or playing, or some such activity, he would have no idea of what he was doing. Somehow, however, behind his confusion he knew he was someone, even when he did not know who he was. Somehow, he knew he loved his wife, who would visit him often, even when he did not know who she was. Somehow, he understood that she was important to him. It caused his wife great distress, because the musician would greet her with great emotion each time he "awoke," as if after a long absence. And, somehow, he knew that there was an "I" that "awoke" to life, one prior to the recovery of his memory.

In short, he was not, even to his wife, solely the sum of his broken, short-lived memories. While the memory clearly has a powerful role in the creation of our identity, and the loss of it deeply affects our sense of who we are, this story and others like it only show how careful we should be in placing too much confidence in memory as the place where our identity exists. We might ask: Who is the "I" that we awake to every morning? Where does *it* reside?

Some have suggested that it is in our free will that our true identity resides. Yet, there are obvious problems here. None of us is completely free to do as we wish. In our daily life we are constantly confronted with limitations as to what we want to do, which is why we get angry when we cannot get what we want. Our boss may tell us to do something we do not want to do. Parents tell their children to study more but the children think they are being pushed too hard. In relationships also, the closer we are to someone, the more we want them to do what we want, and sometimes we get trapped because the other party does not cooperate. We certainly like to say we have free will, but experience tells us otherwise—that we are enmeshed in relationships with others and hidebound in our actions. It seems unlikely, then, that free will is where the self resides.

Perhaps it is with awareness that the self resides. I am aware of things around me, and aware of myself in that environment. Yet, this line of argument also falls down rapidly— especially when we remember the musician above and consider that, in a much less extreme situation, we are not aware of who we are or where we are all the time. For instance, when we sleep our senses are quieted—we do not hear, see, smell, or sense anything. Likewise, people in a coma may not respond to anything. In sleep or in a coma, do we lose our self or our identity?

The Five Aggregates

The questions as to our identity remain, as they have for centuries, open. Certainly, while these questions are intellectually intriguing, they are only of concern to Buddhism in as far as they can alleviate suffering. The suffering of the musician affected with short-term memory was acute, and it was hard for him not to feel enormous frustration at being unable to feel present through time. In a way that most of us can only begin to imagine he lived the condition of impermanence. His identity was only absolute to the extent that at certain moments throughout the day he felt fully aware of himself *for the first time.* But he knew that this condition was itself impermanent and this caused him great distress.

I think this unfortunate man is an example of the central Buddhist teaching of impermanence that the destruction of the World Trade Center made graphically real to all of us. Finding that all those things we thought were permanent— including ourselves and our sense of our self—are, on closer examination, not is deeply frightening. We may feel as though we are disappearing. But Buddhism is not about scaring people; it is, as I have said, about offering solutions. One of the solutions is recognizing impermanence and reconciling oneself to it. Before we do this, however, we need to understand how Buddhism positively conceives of the self.

Buddhism talks about beings. Beings have five aggregates. These aggregates make up the physical body and the mental structure. The aggregates are our physical forms— eyes, ears, nose, tongue, body—our feelings, our perceptions, our volition or willpower, and our consciousness. These aggregates constitute who we are. Buddhism helps us look at what the self is and what being is, and these five aggregates allow us to analyze who we are. When we look at the physique and mentality of a human being, we have already seen how nothing is permanent.

Once more, I do not want to underestimate how difficult this concept may be to grasp. After all, we *feel* as though as we are here. You, the reader, may feel that *you* are reading this book in a chair in your house, and that they are all permanent conditions. And Buddhism does not deny the empirical self. It agrees that you are sitting there and reading this book. Your body, feelings, perceptions, and volition *are* real. What Buddhism adds, however, is that the empirical self is *conditional*. In other words, it is like an onion. The onion is real, but if we peel the onion layer by layer we ultimately cannot find a core. Yet, although there is no core, we cannot deny the existence of the onion. Thus, the onion is conditional. And so are you. And so am I. What makes us present is the aggregation of numerous conditions. This is very important to understand. Non-Self, in Buddhism, does not necessarily mean no-self. The self, in Buddhism, is merely impermanent and interdependent.

Death

I want to emphasize again that grasping the conditionality of the self is not easy—especially when there is suffering. Many people have come to me who are suffering greatly. Sometimes this is because someone they love is dying and they have had to watch them fading away. Sometimes they are dying themselves and are scared. At moments such as these, it is hard to grasp the truth that we are impermanent and that all of us, whether rich or poor, saint or sinner, will have to die. Even when we are confronted by the reality of death, we like to believe we are immortal. It is hard to offer these dying people or their caregivers counsel.

When they come to me, however, I advise these people that, while it is right to be sad at the fact of death, it is important to try and conceive of death in a different manner. Zhuangzi, a Daoist philosopher who lived in China many centuries ago, himself experienced loss when his wife died. Zhuangzi reacted by banging a drum and singing. People around him thought he had gone mad. But he told them that life was a circle of birth and death, and that death was the beginning of a birth. If you did not die, he told them, how could you be reborn? This was why he was celebrating: his wife was going to have a new life.

Zhuangzi was a remarkable man. Not many of us could be as easy-going. Yet, we have to prepare ourselves for the fact that we will die and have to detach ourselves from our sense of our own immortality. We need to be prepared for the fact that life is always changing. Again, this is hard. Not only are we emotionally attached, but we are psychologically attached: we cannot believe that the one we love is dying.

One of the gifts of Buddhism and Chinese culture has been the acceptance of death and the preparation for it. Buddhists prepare for our death every day in order to make it as peaceful as possible. Our temples are very peaceful, havens for people who are frustrated and angered by their jobs and lives. One of the things I always suggest to people is that they try to create a temple everywhere they are. What I mean by this is that we create a peaceful haven for our mind wherever we are. Once in our metaphorical temple we can release the unwholesome thoughts of anger, hatred, frustration, and sadness. We cherish these moments of peace throughout the day.

14

On Safeguarding the Heart
Protecting Ourselves from Losing Our Minds

WHEN WE THINK of the tragedy of September 11 and the suffering that ensued, as well as the suffering that affects so many people around the world in so many different ways, it is sometimes better for a moment to dwell in the moment and let that suffering sit with us. For all of the reality of interdependence, karma, and impermanence that I have discussed in the preceding pages, it would be wrong if we did not recognize how deep and entrenched is suffering in this world. Buddhism, as I have said, is founded on that recognition, and all Buddhists seek in their own ways to alleviate suffering, both for themselves and others. But, as it is necessary to tell ourselves over and over again, none of us should ever underestimate how hard that is to do.

It also would be foolish to underestimate how hard it is for those who are suffering to see a way out. The memories of what happened to bring about that suffering—whether it is the loss of a loved one, physical hunger, a sense of hopelessness—may fade over the course of time; the images of the faces of the loved ones will be frozen in time, their complicated reality simplified by death, their faults forgotten and their lovable qualities enhanced; distractions and new occurrences may dilute the intensity of their absence. The survivors and grieving family and friends may find other partners and friends, or move on, the children will grow, the buildings may be replaced. But their suffering will still be there. It will not go away.

Therefore, for those who are suffering, Buddhism offers a simple counsel that acts as the first point of healing, a kind of triage for the individual: always to safeguard the heart. We need to protect our heart from external or material damage, and from the damage caused by anger, frustration, or fear. We need to protect it as if we were putting a sheet over it. If we do this, we will not get lost.

Anger is a particularly dangerous emotion for the heart. It is a kind of double loss for the grieving or suffering person, because not only have we lost our loved one, but we have lost our heart. Anger works on our hurt feelings, making them even more raw, hurting us more than it hurts the one who caused us pain.

Anger is a natural reaction. For Buddhists, however, the task throughout our lives is to become aware of emotions such as anger and to watch our mind as the emotions well up. Our challenge is to protect our hearts from the damage these emotions can inflict. Anger leads to blind acts of hate—such as when some people after the destruction of the World Trade Center and the Pentagon attacked others because they happened to be Muslim, or look Afghan, or wear hats that reminded people of Afghans. Anger leads people to say, as they did, that they were willing to sacrifice their own lives to kill the people who committed the acts of terror. This cycle of violence only continues the suffering. As someone once said, an eye for an eye leaves the whole world blind. Buddhism does not believe that such acts lead to justice—they merely perpetuate the negative karmic connections. Looking at the events of September 11 from a wider perspective enables us not to excuse the terrorists for what they did but to place this event within a broad context where all of us act, both for good and for bad, in an infinitely complex, interlocking system of cause and effect.

Religious institutions can offer comfort to the broken-hearted, but I always say that it is not so much the temple or church where enlightenment or comfort takes place: it is the mind. This is not to downgrade the importance of religious institutions or the charity they can afford. After all, we need some basic material conditions for reflection to take place: the victim who suffers needs to have physical and material help, and we should rejoice at the generosity that poured out from people around the world in giving money and clothing and blood to the victims of the September 11 tragedy, or any of the countless individual tragedies that occur each day. Moreover, safeguarding the heart is not something we need to be a Buddhist to do. Buddhism is not a secret truth. The truth was always there; it is simply that the Buddha pointed it out.

In order to guard our heart we need to practice awareness. By watching our thoughts and emotions, we can guard against literally losing our mind. Earlier, I briefly mentioned controlling the oxen of the mind. Practicing awareness is like an ox herder watching his oxen. He needs to keep an eye on his oxen or they will wander off beyond his fields. We need to control our mind so it does not become wild. Indeed, the very act of watching the mind can bring it back into balance. Balance is very important here. If there is too much sorrow in our mind, we need to bring some kind of joy into it to balance it. When there is too much levity, we need to make it more serene and calm. When we are very angry, we need to cool the mind down. When the mind is indifferent, we need to bring more life to it.

In order for us to balance the mind it is important to know what our mental state is. Many of us who let the mind go wild do not know we are unhappy or angry or depressed. We have not taken time to monitor our mental state. So the first thing we need to do is to know our state of mind. This is why I say it is necessary to guard our heart from anger. Until we know what we are feeling, how can we protect ourselves from the consequences of that feeling?

The point of knowing what we are feeling is not to deny those feelings. Anger is a genuine emotion; stifling it will not give us any relief. It will merely emerge in some other direction. Yet, if we observe the anger, that act in and of itself will provide some sense of how we deal with the emotion. And one of the great lessons of Buddhism is the use of meditation to do just that.

15 ❧
On Mental Anguish
Stilling the Disordered Mind

MEDITATION OFFERS AN opportunity to still mental anguish through the safeguarding of our heart from negative emotions. Meditation is like a security guard monitoring who is coming in and going out of a building. Meditation observes the thoughts—whether they are good, bad, or neutral. Buddhism has two kinds of meditation, which are really part of the same process. One is called *Samadhi* and the other is *Vipassana*. In Chinese, we call the first the meditation on calmness and stillness; the second we call the meditation on insight and contemplation.

To use an analogy I employed earlier on in this book, Samadhi meditation practice involves allowing the glass of murky water to be stilled and the sediment to settle. In other words, disturbed feelings that cloud our reason and confuse our sense of what we need to do should be allowed to calm down so that our reason becomes clearer and the way forward more transparent. By watching our anger, for instance, we can actually help control it, simply by acknowledging that we are watching it. Meditation allows us not to be overwhelmed by the emotion and instead to ask ourselves what we are angered by, whom we are angry with, and why. Vipassana meditation then follows up these questions by asking how the anger comes to happen and why it is affecting us. We are then able to ask how the anger is helping or disabling us and how we can let it go away.

Both forms of meditation need to work together. If we are overwhelmed by anger, we will not be able to ask how the anger happens and why it is affecting us. We will be so wrapped up in the emotion—in wanting to hurt someone or to hurt ourselves—that we will not care why we are feeling what we are feeling. We will not want to hear any other options, even the ones that are speaking to us from our gut. So, the calmness and stillness brought about by the first form of meditation are essential for the emotions to be quieted so that they cannot overwhelm us. Once the mind is stilled, it is possible to answer the questions of the second stage.

Thus, in the case of the terrorist attack on the World Trade Center and the Pentagon, only when we have calmed ourselves can we ask the questions: Why were those people killed? Why did the murderers act the way they did? Why did those victims die? Why did this happen? What will happen to me in the future? How are we going to deal with our anger? Will anger help us? I like to think of these two meditative functions as a mirror. In the first form, we polish the mirror so that we can see things clearly, which is a function of the second form of meditation. The mirror that we polish not only reflects back to us things we did not see clearly because we had not disciplined the mind, but it opens up the areas behind us so we can see more clearly the causes and effects of our feelings. Moreover, with a polished mirror we no longer only see things narrowly. We can look at the mirror from any angle, opening up to our view more visions previously hidden from us. We can ask ourselves about the September 11 terrorists: Why did they come? Why did they use the objects they used to cause terror? What is our responsibility?

When we have gone through the process of stilling and then examining the mind, what occurs is not indifference but compassion. This is activated by our sense of karma, of how we are all linked together. It is very important for us to realize that everybody in society should try to create good karma. Once we realize our interconnectedness, that all things have an effect, both long- and short-term, and that things we do, individually and collectively, may reverberate in ways we could not have imagined because we remained blinkered by our own cultural, religious, or other conditioning, then we can all contribute toward the relief of suffering. The wound that another individual experiences becomes our wound, their suffering our suffering. Likewise, our healing becomes their healing, the alleviation of our suffering the alleviation of theirs.

In such circumstances, therefore, not only does the suffering person need healing, but we all need healing—and it is everyone's responsibility to undertake that healing. However, if we focus solely on individual cases and ignore the larger connection, and consequently consider revenge as the only option for action, then we will cause more hatred and more hurt—to ourselves and others. In the same way, if we merely try to excise the wound without realizing how it came about, then we will spread the infection to other parts so that the wound becomes worse.

Such a response has clear implications for how we deal with the aftermath of events like the September 11 tragedies. We can try to look at such an event as an isolated incident and thus perpetuate a cycle of murder and revenge, a cycle of birth–death–rebirth that represents the pain of reincarnation's vicious circle. In turn, this is how Buddhism understands the immediate punishments for bad deeds: wrongdoers collect enough bad karma when they die that they are punished by reincarnation in a bad realm of heaven. Or we can look at the event from a holistic perspective and chart a course that has a better chance of creating less anger and fewer wounds in the future—thus saving us all more pain and suffering.

16 ❦
On Faith
The Distortion between Religion and Faith

I THINK IT will be helpful to further explore the issue of punishment for those who do bad things. To contemporary Buddhists such as myself, the idea of realms of heaven seems a somewhat archaic way of trying to understand what happens to people who did bad things before they died. The way I see it making sense to people today is to say that the murderer is also the victim of his own bad energy—his unhappiness, his disturbed mind, and his hatred are in themselves forms of punishment.

I do not believe that the World Trade Center bombers were happy. I do not believe they were content with the world around them. They may have genuinely believed they were going to heaven and that the Islam they believed in sanctioned their behavior. But I think their very acts prove them wrong. Islam does not offer that kind of salvation and they will not end up in heaven. Their failure to still their own minds in life may have foreshadowed the lack of stillness they will have after death.

Some people may conceive that, because it believes in karma and stillness, Buddhism teaches passivity and acceptance of evil rather than actively trying to stop it. This is wrong. Buddhism recognizes that while we—by which I mean the human race—are the same, we are also different. We live in different spheres with different influences, even though those influences are interconnected. There are some people who want to destroy other people, and they need to be stopped.

From a Buddhist perspective, stopping people from making bad karma is necessary. A Mahayana Buddhist text entitled the Upaya-kausalya Sutra depicts a bodhisattva sea captain named Maha Karuna who, in order to save the other five hundred passengers, has to kill a robber who is trying to murder all the people on the boat. This may shock those who believe that Buddhism only advocates nonviolence. Even in such extreme situations, in which many lives will be spared if one is taken, the karma that Maha Karuna will take on himself will be a heavy one. And that is exactly the point. The bodhisattva needs to take responsibility for the result of negative karma caused by his action against the robber. He is aware of that burden, and of the need for wisdom and awareness of the consequences that will flow from his actions. The question remains: For those of us who are not bodhisattvas and do not consider our actions as deeply as the captain, what kind of action is considered appropriate?

Killing bad people may destroy particular individuals, but it does not get rid of the causes or the results of the individuals' actions. It is, in other words, only a short-term solution. As we have seen over and over again, killing one person can generate many future killers who see that one person as a martyr. This is at heart what has caused the turmoil in Afghanistan and has led to murder and bloodshed in the Middle East.

Buddhism itself balances such individual action with a recognition that we are all connected, all dependent. We always need to remind ourselves of this connection, and to look for ways in which it manifests itself. Buddhism is very practical and realistic about motivation and outcome. Two stories told by the Buddha highlight how realistic Buddhism is when it comes to establishing right and wrong behavior.

At the time of the Buddha, there was a prince called Jeta, who had received the five precepts from the Buddha: not to kill, not to steal, not to be sexually promiscuous or wanton, not to lie, and not to drink intoxicants. The prince, however, was finding the fifth one hard to keep, because as a prince he led a very social life. So the prince went to the Buddha and told him he did not want to uphold the five precepts. "I want to change," he said.

"When you drink are you really happy?" the Buddha asked.

"No, I am always worrying about the five precepts."

"Do not worry," the Buddha said. "Because your mind is not indulgent when you drink you are, therefore, not violating the five precepts."

We call this the "leaky good"—like a leaky roof. It is an imperfect good, but a good nonetheless, because the prince has not allowed his mind to become indulgent.

Another story the Buddha told concerns the Empress Malika. Malika's husband, the Emperor, was very hungry but did not like the chef's food. So much did he dislike the food that he threatened to have the chef taken out and beheaded. When Malika, who had received the five precepts, heard of this she prepared a meal and dressed herself in her most gorgeous clothes. Accompanying the Emperor, she invited him for a drink and to feast. The Emperor was surprised.

"You observe the five precepts," he said. "Why today are you deciding to drink?"

"I am in a good mood and wish for your company in enjoying this wine and food," she replied.

The Emperor, after he had dined with the Empress, turned to her and said, "This food is not good. Where is my chef?" Then he realized he had given orders for him to be killed and regretted his haste. The Empress then told him that she had protected the cook and that he was not dead. Far from being angry at Malika's deception, the Emperor was delighted that his order had not been carried out. The Empress had performed an imperfect good, breaking one precept in order to save someone's life.

What these stories show is that living in this world and alleviating the suffering of others is always challenging, for it may involve compromises with one's own sense of right and wrong. Nevertheless, Buddhism demands action. It demands it even when we are not able to conduct ourselves with absolute probity in all aspects of our life. Since Buddhism believes we are all connected, it does not believe that anyone is truly perfect, because karma binds us all together. The bodhisattva vow is one that seeks out suffering and seeks to remedy it. It does not expect us to dwell on our own self-righteousness or lock ourselves away from the realities of life.

This is why we need to be humble about our responses to evil doings. We need to reflect on their causes, without attachment and blame. We need, reasonably and responsibly, to take on the bad karma ourselves and see how we in some way might have been to blame for some aspects of the tragedy that has befallen us. In sum, we need to think about the laws of cause and effect. When September 11 occurred, Billy Graham told people that he did not know where God had been. Buddhist Master Hsing Yun, however, did: "God," he said, "is in the laws of cause and effect."

That said, we should be aware of the pressure on us, and the pressure we place on others, to alleviate suffering. Sometimes we burden ourselves too greatly. This only weighs us down and thus, paradoxically, makes us less able to help the alleviation of suffering. When I think about this, I think about a green apple on a tree. The apple possesses the final shape it is going to be; it is even the same size, but it is not ripe. Sometimes we need to sit and let time work its course for something to come to fruition. We are often so impatient to have things done or brought to completion—even when we are acting against the natural, physical laws of the universe.

There is a story about a Buddhist sage that shows how we carry burdens around with us. One day, the sage and a disciple came to a riverbank where a young woman was trying to cross. She was unable to walk through the swollen tide and asked the sage to help. In spite of his vows not to touch women, the sage picked up the woman and carried her across the river on his back. Once they had reached the other side of the river, the sage lowered the woman to the ground. She thanked him profusely and bade him farewell.

The disciple was shocked by the sage's breaking of his vow, but said nothing. After three months, the disciple could stand it no more. He went to the sage and reproached him for breaking his vow by touching a woman. The sage laughed: "I merely carried the burden of this woman for the length of time it took to cross a river; yet you have been burdened by it for more than three months. Who has been more errant from his vows?"

What this story tells us is that we cannot freight our deeds with meaning when the meaning itself will weigh us down. If we do good, we need to act without expectations of reward or revenge or recognition. If we do so, the karma of our thoughts will not go against the karma of our deeds.

17 ❦
On the Four Diligences
Paths to Tranquility

B EFORE DETAILING THE power of meditation as a
practical method to help relieve suffering, I need to
point out the Four Diligences, which are key components of
meditation. An essential feature of meditation is the disci-
plining of the mind. Buddhism achieves this through practices based on what are called the Four Diligences. Of the
Four Diligences, two deal with good thoughts, and two with
bad. Both of them are balanced contrasts, although in practice they are deeply interwoven.

The first diligence is to prevent bad thoughts from
arising in the first place. The second diligence is to deal with
the bad thoughts once they have arisen by eliminating them.
The third diligence is to generate good thoughts if they have

not arisen, while the fourth diligence is to nourish those good thoughts if they have arisen and make them stronger and more substantial. The Four Diligences are directly applicable to the ego and desire. Our relationships are often begun out of desire; perhaps we know a relationship will not work but want to try it for a short time to see what it will be like. Many times we pay for our indulgence. We need to have the strength and self-knowledge to examine our thoughts as they arise to see what desires, cravings, attachments, or impulses lie behind them and whether they are good or bad thoughts.

These diligences apply not only to human relationships but to our relationships with all things. For instance, some people tell me I am a high-tech nun because I use computers. I like using faxes, digital cameras, camcorders, cellular phones, and other mechanical objects because they are efficient and make our life easier. But I do not want machines to rule our lives or make life more complicated through our reliance on them. We have to remember that we invented the machines and not they us!

One of the central problems, I believe, in contemporary society is that we do not practice the Four Diligences enough. We rush headlong into acquiring things, relationships, and technology without wondering whether we really need them or want them for our own selfish purposes rather than generating good. I understand that talk about the dissolute life tends to be filled with clichés—drugs, women, marital problems, the high life. Unfortunately, however, there is some truth in clichés. Rarely do we want to count the true costs of our attachments and desires, but this is what we must do in order to create good consequences and good karma, and to avoid the reverse.

How do we apply the Four Diligences to something such as anger? When we encounter something that upsets us, we tell ourselves not to let the anger hurt us first. You may have received a letter in which somebody slanders or rejects you. Or your lover may have written you a letter to say that he or she is breaking up with you. Therefore, you get angry. The first thing we need to do is to keep ourselves calm and give ourselves constructive thoughts. We keep ourselves calm by not allowing the disturbing thoughts to arise or, should we begin to feel ourselves getting angry, by diverting those angry thoughts and, as it were, unattaching ourselves from them. We tell ourselves we are not going to let the anger hurt us.

The second step is to tell ourselves that we are going to deal with this matter calmly and wisely. In order to do this, we need to have positive and wholesome thoughts inside us before dealing with the outside matter. Sometimes, it may not be enough to tell ourselves to stop being angry. The anger may not disappear that easily. If we need to go shopping or listen to music, then that is fine. But the *thought* behind the action is very important. We must not let the anger hurt us. We must think calmly and wisely.

Buddhist understanding of who we are and what our relationship is to the outside world is particularly useful in helping us deal with anger. Frustration occurs because we are not aware of, and are not prepared for, change. When we get frustrated with our relationships, our family, school, society, our financial status, and career, it is often because everything is changing. Therefore, Buddhism teaches the concept of dependent origination—of everything involved with everything else. I could not have done the things I have done without others. Nor could you. If we only saw life in this way, we would be able to appreciate how much we have.

Dealing with our thoughts requires awareness, before any action can take place. I always say that the mind is our fate. Some people when they encounter frustration are able to reconstruct their thoughts as to how they became frustrated in the first place. But many of us allow the mind and our thoughts to overwhelm us, to lead us wherever they like. We need to be aware of our thoughts, so that when they are good we can let them flourish but when they are bad we can remove them. They are like a seed planted in the ground. If it is left alone, the seed will tend to flourish and grow. If the seed is good, then it is all right. But if the seed is bad then we need to uproot it. However, the best method is to be aware that the thought is bad at the beginning, before it is planted. Otherwise, if we are not aware and let the thought grow like a big tree and then try to get rid of it, the task is much harder. Not only do we have to chop off the branches and cut through the trunk, but we still have to deal with the roots that need to be dug out. And this is how habits and addictions are formed. We may get rid of the visible manifestation of our bad thoughts, but we have not addressed the root causes of those thoughts. Consequently, soon enough, the bad thoughts begin to sprout again.

18 🦎

Meditation

Breathing and Stillness

MEDITATION INVOLVES DISCIPLINE and training. Because we live in a world where we are so easily distracted, where our mind is always wandering around outside our heads, as it were, it may take some time and effort to learn to control the oxen! We are bombarded by images that stimulate our minds into frenzied activities. The first act of meditation should be to remove ourselves from external stimulation and draw the mind inward. This step is then followed by the meditator asking him- or herself a fundamental question: "What are you thinking?" Observe yourself and your thoughts. Examine what thoughts you are thinking, what is in your mind at that moment. The idea at this point is not necessarily to change those thoughts but merely to examine what they are. This is called cultivating awareness, and it is the essential mechanism of meditation. One further statement that needs to be made before I discuss the processes of meditation is that meditation does not mean sitting down in a temple or a church. It can be done anywhere, even when we are walking along. At every moment during the day, we can ask ourselves what we are thinking. Nevertheless, given that most people when they think about meditation think it is about sitting still, I will concentrate on sitting meditation. As a basic technique, sitting meditation is, indeed, extremely effective.

There are three elements to meditation. The first element is body posture. We need to sit erect but relaxed. We might cross our legs fully in the lotus position, or if we are not yet supple enough for this position we may sit in the half-lotus position. I recommend the latter for those who are older or for people in physical discomfort. It is important that we feel comfortable and relaxed.

When we are in this position, we should do an inventory of our body from the top of our head to the bottom of our toes and check each part of the body to make sure every muscle is relaxed. First we should relax the top of the head and then the forehead. If we are frowning, release the frown. If our cheeks are tense, then smile a little. Place our tongue against the roof of the mouth behind the teeth. Open or close our eyes as we wish, as long as closing our eyes will not make us drowsy. The important thing is to become aware and not fall asleep! Then we should concentrate on following all of the muscles down the body, placing our mind in each area of the body and checking to see whether the muscles are relaxed or tense. We join our palms together, with the tips of our thumbs connecting and the fingers interlaced and sit upright, not in a fixed, rigid position but comfortably. Our spine should be straight and not hunched over.

The second element in meditation is breathing. A standard technique for breathing is counting each breath as it goes in and out. On the first in- and out-breath we should count to one. On the second in- and out-breath we should count to two. On the third, we should count to three, and so on up to ten. Then we should return to one, and then two, etc. The more slowly we can do this, the better, although we shouldn't try and force ourselves beyond our natural breathing patterns. Once again, the point is not to hold our breath but to become conscious of our breathing. It is preferable to allow the fresh air that is breathed in through the lungs to go right into the abdomen and then to bring the stale breath from inside the body out through the nose.

The next element of the breathing technique is to focus on the breathing itself. We should be aware of the air as it enters our nostrils and goes down into the body and then as it comes back out of the body. Do not try and breathe in too much air or make too much of an effort. Simply breathing rhythmically and consciously is already awareness in action and will aid us in our concentration. We can use this technique to quell our anger or to safeguard our heart, or even when we are nervous because we are meeting someone important or are about to do something dangerous. By not letting our mind get distracted and focusing on the breathing, we can lower our heart rate, oxygenate the blood, and let our mind rest for a while.

By observing our breathing we are automatically controlling our thought patterns. This is the third element of meditation. Controlling thought patterns is all about avoiding distractions and learning to concentrate. To do this, we need to be aware of breathing and focus on certain bodily sensations.

The effect can be extraordinary. When I became a nun, twenty-three years ago, I had an ulcer. An endoscopy revealed that I had two small holes in the lining of my stomach. One night, the pain was excruciating and I sat up and began to meditate. After adjusting my posture and beginning to breathe consciously I began to focus on the two holes. I brought all my energy to bear on them. I tried to pinpoint the pain, moving my mind around the area where it had hurt. The strange thing was that the more I examined the area the more I realized that the pain was moving. I couldn't pinpoint the exact source. In addition, I was trying to work out what I felt exactly—what the nature of the pain was. We often say that we feel pain, but we often cannot describe what the pain really is. I wanted to find out the essence of the pain.

So as I sat and tried not only to locate the pain but to determine its nature, I discovered that the pain had vanished. What I had realized was that the pain was conditioned, and that once I had brought my focus to the pain, the pain had revealed itself to be nothing in and of itself and had gone. I had peeled away each layer of pain until there was nothing at the core. After that meditation, I cured the ulcer, and I have not taken medicine for twenty-three years.

Now, while this discovery was extraordinary for me, it was not miraculous. In fact, it was profoundly rational. My thought was: I have two holes in the wall of my stomach; I need to mend them. I used my thoughts and their energies as a kind of healing medication to mend the holes. In Chinese acupuncture, practitioners talk of the "acupuncture of the will." What they mean is that, while the doctors may use physical needles to stimulate the energy that might heal the wound, the other needle that has to be employed for healing to take place is the will.

Meditation has the power to activate the will and focus it very effectively. I am not advocating its suitability for all ailments, especially very serious diseases or illnesses, but the focused mind is a powerful tool. Meditation will not stop suffering—as we have seen, nothing can. However, meditation can provide us with a way to lessen the by-products of suffering, such as anger, frustration, or fear. In such a way, meditation enables us to look more clearly upon the causes of suffering and spend our lives dedicated to lessening it— for ourselves and for all sentient beings.

Conclusion ❦
After September 11

SEPTEMBER 11 WAS not the first tragedy to strike humanity and it will not be the last. It was not the gravest event and it was not the most inconsequential. Yet numbers and comparisons can never take away the individual loss that individuals suffered—and all of us who were in some way touched by what happened that day must honor that. For me, September 11 is an encapsulation of suffering, emblematic of the causes and effects of violence in extraordinary circumstances and in our day-to-day lives. It encompasses for me the choices we can make in deciding on the direction of our lives and the country.

Buddhism does not offer easy solutions or emotional palliatives. Instead, it realistically responds to suffering—both in our own lives and in the lives of others—and demands that we do something about it. It does so in compassion and with the recognition that we are far from perfect; it does so acknowledging that we will never be perfect while we think we *can* be perfect. Buddhism can be harsh; but then so can pain, and so can responsibility. We cannot merely hope for suffering to end or wait around for others to end it for us. If we do, we will be hoping in vain and waiting for an eternity. Buddhism provides a way of engaging that promises liberation for all of us because our destinies are bound up with all the other beings who share this planet—whether they be our families, those who seek to destroy our way of life, those who rescue us from the flames, or those countless others whose names and lives we will never know.

As I hope this book has shown, September 11 teaches us that life is very fragile and precious, that our time on this earth demands not resignation or forgetfulness but mindfulness and engagement. It teaches us that there is beauty even in the midst of horror, but only if we work for the good of all rather than the particular interests of the few. It asks us to commit to what seems impossible—a life dedicated to the helping of others who do not belong to our family but to the family of Man, and then beyond that to the families of all beings who live and die and live again on this small blue orb in the three layers of the thousand worlds.

Appendix *
Humanistic Buddhism

IN 1979, A friend took me to a Buddhist monastery in my native Taiwan for a retreat. I saw it more as an opportunity to have a vacation, with free board and lodging, and thought no more of it. However, the monastery—the Fo Guang Shan temple—taught me meditation and chanting, and helped me realize that Buddhism was not superstitious or for old people, as I had previously thought, but was practical and contemporary. I joined as soon as I could and through the institution undertook further studies in law and Buddhist philosophy, and I have been with the temple, both in the United States and Taiwan, ever since.

Fo Guang Shan's founder was Master Hsing Yun, who became a Buddhist monk at age of twelve and fled to Taiwan from mainland China in 1949 and founded the Fo Guang

Shan International Buddhist Order soon afterwards. There are now hundreds of temples all over the world, including Asia, the United States, Europe, Central and South America, Africa and Australia. Although we practice Chan Buddhism (the Chinese form of Zen Buddhism), Master Hsing Yun has named his particular school Humanistic Buddhism.

Humanistic Buddhism has six main characteristics. The first is its emphasis on the human nature of the Buddha. Sakyamuni Buddha, the founder of Buddhism, was a living human being, born in this world, with a family, and a real life. He attained his enlightenment in this world. He is not a divine being or the creator. He proclaimed that he was a discoverer who found the path which shared by the ancient sages as well. Humanistic Buddhism emphasizes the Buddha's humanity because it shows that we can all be compassionate, ethical, and use intuitive wisdom as he did.

The second characteristic is Humanistic Buddhism's emphasis on daily life. The Buddha gave very specific instructions on how we should live our daily life, and Humanistic Buddhism advocates following those instructions. We experience the suffering in our daily life and we need to eliminate it in our everyday life. The wisdom is to apply the Buddhist value and ethic in our daily life.

The third characteristic is altruism—that we always keep in mind how we can help and best serve others. We cannot live isolatedly when the Buddha taught us the interdependence of all beings. A Buddha, the enlightened one, cannot reach his goal by separating himself from all the sentient beings. We cannot reach our happiness while the rest of the world is suffering.

The fourth characteristic is joyfulness. Our aim is to provide joy through the relief of suffering for all sentient beings. The goal for Buddhists is the cessation of the suffering. It is very important to bring joy not only to one's own self but also to others. Meditation and contemplation are used to eliminate the negative thoughts with which we harm ourselves.

The fifth characteristic is timeliness. Humanistic Buddhism seeks to make Buddhism meaningful and relevant for today's spiritual seekers. We adopt the values and principles of Buddhism to examine the current social issues and advocate peaceful, non-violent solutions. Humanistic Buddhism works to build a heaven-like pure land on this earth. When we take good care in this life, this moment, we are not worried about the life after death.

The sixth characteristic is universality. The wisdom of the Buddha is not under the exclusive control of a group of people, nor does his wisdom only apply to a few. It applies to all beings, because he wished to save all beings. Humanistic Buddhism believes that all the sentient beings embrace the potential for enlightenment, regardless of social status, race, gender, or even species.

Humanistic Buddhism provides a dynamic form of contemporary Buddhism that promotes compassion and wisdom, is practical in orientation, and is open to everyone, no matter their background or religious affiliation. For more information, contact: Greater Boston Buddhist Cultural

Center, 950 Massachusetts Avenue, Cambridge, MA 02139. Tel: 617-547-6670; fax: 617-868-1189, Web: www.gbbcc.org; e-mail: info@gbbcc.org.